MARY FITZ

Ten Minutes a Day

READINGS AND REFLECTIONS FOR EACH DAY OF LENT

THE COLUMBA PRESS
DUBLIN 1992

First edition, 1992, published by
THE COLUMBA PRESS
93, The Rise, Mount Merrion, Blackrock, Co Dublin, Ireland

Cover by Bill Bolger
Origination by The Columba Press
Printed by Colour Books, Dublin

ISBN: 1 85607 040 9

The author gratefully acknowledges the help and inspiration of Mr R. Knightly, Brother Ramon SSF, Rev D. Lawrence, Sister Edna Monica SLG, Miss M. Meyerkort, Miss H. Thom, Mrs D. Eynon, Mr and Mrs B. Fitzgerald, Brother David Jardine SSF, Rev Canon G. Edwards, Captain C. Dronsfield CA, Mrs M. Seelig, Miss C. Davis, Mr and Mrs R. Mehta.

Scripture citations are normally from the NEB, with occasional usages from the Authorised Version and the NIV. Other quotations are taken from the following and are used by permission: *Alternative Service Book 1980, Praying Together,* by P. Caraman (CTS and SPCK), *The Art of Loving* by Eric Fromm (Unwin), *Enfolded in Love* (DLT), *Every Day is a Gift* (CBC, New York), *A People's Life of Christ* by J. Paterson-Smyth (Hodder and Stoughton), *Songs of Praise* (OUP), and *Transformed by Love* by Margaret Magdalen (DLT).

Copyright © 1992, Mary Fitzgerald

Contents

Week of Ash Wednesday   4
This is my Son, my Beloved

1st Week of Lent   12
I am the alpha and the omega

2nd Week of Lent   26
I am the light of the world

3rd Week of Lent   40
I am the Good Shepherd

4th Week of Lent   54
I am the True Vine

5th Week of Lent   68
I am the Bread of Life

6th Week of Lent   82
Behold the Lamb of God

Ash Wednesday

I saw the Spirit coming down from heaven like a dove and resting upon him. (Jn 1: 32)

Reading: Mt 3:1-17

This was the beginning. It was for this that his body and mind, his soul and spirit had been prepared. This was his destiny, that which would bring humankind closer to God in spirit. In a life which had begun with an angel's message and had meant years of self preparation, this was the moment to move forward. The time was now upon him.

He made his way through the crowd to the man standing in the river. 'Repent; for the kingdom of heaven is upon you!' The man, in a coat of camel's hair, increased his cry: 'I baptise you with water, for repentance; but the one who comes after me is mightier than I. I am not fit to take off his shoes.' Another person stepped into the river to be baptised. The man scooped up water and poured it over the person's head. 'He will baptise you with the Holy Spirit and with fire.' The baptiser's eyes burned with fervour, his body exuded vigour and enthusiasm. He looked over towards the bank and noticed the other standing there, distinctive in the midst of the crowd. Silently he stood there, the One who had been at the heart of the baptiser's vision, held for many years, the One who was the fulfilment of his life's purpose: 'and you, my child, you shall be called Prophet of the Highest, for you will be the Lord's forerunner to prepare his way and lead his people to salvation through knowledge of him, by the forgiveness of their sins.' (Lk 1: 76-77) Quieted by the presence of the One whom he instinctively recognised, John asked, 'Do you come to me? I need rather to be baptised by you.' Jesus replied, 'Let it be so for the present.'

And so, by means of the baptism by John, the symbolic gesture of cleansing and purification through which the latter had helped many put behind them their old ways and start afresh, came Jesus to his appointed time. This was the moment when, empowered by the in-pouring of the Spirit of God, he would become the bridge which would reconnect humanity more strongly with its Creator. He came up out of the water, 'This is my Son, my Beloved, on whom my favour rests.'

So Jesus offers himself to be symbolically cleansed with water by John, along with all the other people, before being empowered by the Holy Spirit. In this he demonstrates his oneness with them, with humanity even though, being without sin, he has no need of purification. Christ Jesus joins himself to humanity through this symbolic act, taking within himself all aspects of their humanness, and becoming one with them on this level. But with the in-pouring of the Holy Spirit he is also gathered into oneness with God. Thus he is both at one with God and at one with humanity, becoming the bridge linking the two. Christ Jesus is still our bridge, our link between our life on this earth and our life in God as God's children. 'No one comes to the Father except by me.' (Jn 14: 6) By giving himself into John's hands to be baptised, to be symbolically cleansed, before his anointing with the Spirit, he shows us that before we can truly experience a life in God and empowerment by his Spirit, we have to be cleansed and purified. Our lives on earth are in part a process of cleansing and purification, a 'taming' of our lower natures by our higher ones so that the former are not in direct control of us. We have been given the opportunity to be awakened in our spiritual lives, to allow the workings of our higher natures to prevail. The means by which this can take place is through Christ Jesus. He can be the one who cleanses us so that God's Spirit might begin to work more strongly and effectively within us, might begin to empower and enable us. And he can be the bridge between ourselves and God, infusing and indwelling our higher selves so that they can permeate and transform our lower ones, and thus our lives.

So the Word became flesh; he came to dwell among us, and we saw his glory.

Thursday after Ash Wednesday

Jesus was then led away by the Spirit into the wilderness. (Mt 4:1)
Reading: Lk 4: 1-2

Jesus withdrew into the wilderness. It was the beginning of his mission. He needed to think things over after the baptism in the Jordan by John, and the overlighting by the Holy Spirit – 'this is my beloved Son.' (Mt 3:17) He needed time and space to reflect upon the enormity of the task that he was about to take on.

The words 'Jesus withdrew' come often in the Gospels. (Mt 14: 13; Mk 2: 35-36; Lk 4: 42; Jn 12:40) He withdrew to think; to make commitment to God (in the wilderness) ; to come to major decisions (in the Garden of Gethsemane); to rest his mind, body and spirit in God's presence; to be nourished and revitalised. Many times did he become weary through healing and preaching – large groups of people sapping his energy and strength. Even he could not continuously meet the constant demands of the people around him without times of peace and revitalisation. So he withdrew to 'recharge his batteries' into the peace of the hillsides, the lakeside, away from everyone, where he could be alone with God. He could just 'be' in God's presence.

If Jesus himself felt the need, often, to withdraw and be quiet with God, how much more so do we have this need. We who do not have the same inner resources. Many of us do not allow ourselves enough time or space to 'rest inwardly'. If we give of ourselves continuously we can become drained of our inner strength and resources, and illness can be the result. Stress, according to the medical profession, is one of the major factors in diseases such as cancer, and now vast numbers of people need medically prescribed sleeping aids. Relaxation classes are now offered to help prevent stress-related disease or alleviate its symptoms. Clearly there is an imbalance in our present way of life and a need to withdraw from our daily pressures to somewhere where we can find inner peace and rest.

Walking used to be a good disperser of pressure, giving space and time for 'resting and reflecting inwardly' as the body relaxed in gentle exercise. But, with more rapid travelling in cars and 'no time' to walk (time is never on our side), that opportunity has lessened.

THIS IS MY SON, MY BELOVED

We need to explore all the possibilities of withdrawal in our lives. For Jesus it meant being alone in quiet places in the countryside, away from the anxieties and problems of others; space to breath, be at peace and think without distraction; absorbing the beauty of his surroundings and allowing his whole body and mind to rest and soak up the quietness. But more importantly it meant the opportunity to be in close communion with God. 'But for him there was a deeper need than bodily repose. Before dawn, "a great while before day" Peter heard him steal out of the house ... With the golden dawn touching the hilltops and the lake in its silent beauty lying below, Peter found him kneeling on the brown hillside, resting his soul in undisturbed communion with the Father. That was his constant need in all his earthly life. Even he could not go for long without it.' (*A People's Life of Christ*)

Some of us choose to commune with God on 'retreat', relaxing and being close to him in peaceful surroundings, with spiritual guidance available if required. Some take the opportunities offered by travel agents to 'get away from it all', communing peacefully with God whilst exploring his beautiful world. But even just withdrawing and being quiet with God for a few minutes each day can afford us great benefit. We can experience the inner peace and stillness, the richness and quiet of his presence, and in these moments he can and will refresh, revitalise and nourish us so that we feel rested and strengthened in our inner selves.

Be still and know that I am God.

Friday after Ash Wednesday

It had been said, 'You are not to put the Lord your God to the test.' (Lk 4:12)

Reading: Mt 4: 2-11

So Jesus spends forty days and nights alone, fasting in the wilderness, contemplating his future, his capability to undertake the enormous task ordained for him and the challenges it would bring. Here, when in his most vulnerable state, the devil comes to tempt him.

The devil attacks the humanness of Jesus three times, potential weak spots that could be worked upon and exploited, those same ones that are in each one of us. The first is the challenge to Jesus to use his power for his own ends, in this case to ease his hunger. Jesus withstands this, stressing that spiritual rather than physical nourishment is more important. The devil then attacks a second area, that of fear, doubt and lack of trust. He challenges Jesus to test God's declared commitment to and love for him, but again Jesus withstands the provocation. Finally, the devil makes his assault on the area of human greed for power, control and domination. He offers Jesus, 'all the kingdoms of the world in their glory' in return for his obeisance. Jesus again withstands the temptation and firmly sends the devil away. The latter had tried to disempower Jesus by undermining his belief and trust in God, and in his own integrity. But it is the devil himself who is ultimately disempowered. Jesus even under extreme duress with his physical strength depleted, calls upon his inner strength and resources, withstands the testing and wins through.

We all have our own personal 'devils' which come to tempt, to test or to disempower us, appearing at those moments of weakness which assail us at times. One major one is doubt. Even the most resolute of us can fall prey to doubt and fear when under extreme pressure. We hear those voices inside which seek to undermine our belief in ourselves, our abilities to carry out certain tasks or to cope with certain situations. We hear those which tell us that God has forgotten us, is no longer there to sustain us when we most need him and that we can no longer trust him. Even the greatest people can be touched by doubt and fear.

Consider John the Baptist, the strong, forceful proclaimer of Christ Jesus. Even he, confined in the discomfort, solitude and restraint of prison, began to doubt Jesus' authenticity, finally being forced to send for confirmation via messengers. (Lk 7: 19-23) He who, during his lifetime, had held his vision firmly before him now became bewildered by the slowness of events and by Jesus' apparent unwillingness to declare himself. His discomfort, his deprived condition weighed upon him causing him to doubt Jesus' credibility. However, Jesus understood, completely aware of John's situation, the agony of spirit, mind and body that the confinement caused him and what suffering of that kind can do to the mental, physical and emotional stamina of the strongest people. So he sent a message to John that was full of reassurance and hope. For he had experienced his own time of doubt and physical suffering in the wilderness and he knew how quick the devil had been to jump in and take advantage of this, assailing him with temptation at his weakest moments. So, as Jesus had the beguiling voice of the tempter to test his inner strength, John had doubt and depression to test his.

Christ Jesus understands how the bravest spirit can be crushed into doubt, fear and denial under torture, oppression and cruelty, even those with the surest of faith. He has supreme compassion for those who are tortured or victimised for their beliefs, kept in solitary confinement or held ransom by oppressors through threats to their lives and those of their loved ones. He understands if their spiritedness or their faith is weakened as a result. But he also has compassion and understanding for those of us who are held to ransom by our own phobias, tortured by the scars of our experiences and oppressed or isolated through the manifestations of our own insecurities. Just as he sent messages of reassurance and hope to John in prison, so he constantly sends us that same message; that he is with us in all situations, however bleak they may seem, and at all times; that however much we are assailed by doubts and fears, temptations or tests, we can always hold on to him – our hope, our support, our steadfast friend.

Great is Our Lord, and of great power,
His understanding is infinite. (Ps 47)

Saturday after Ash Wednesday
The Spirit of the Lord is upon me because he has anointed me. (Lk 4: 18)
Reading: Lk 4:14-20

So Jesus returns to Nazareth after his empowerment by the Spirit and his testing in the wilderness at the beginning of his ministry. In the synagogue he reads aloud a prophecy from Isaiah and announces that now this prophecy, in the hearing of all those there, has been fulfilled. However, this is not acceptable to the Nazarenes and he is turned out of his home town. So for Jesus this was both a beginning and an end. It was the end of his old life, his time of growing up and preparation, and it was the beginning of his new one, the start of his ministry of teaching and healing. It was also the end of the 'old order', the covenant given by God to Abraham (Gen 17: 1-21) and the beginning of the new covenant (Mt 26:29-29), God's sending of the Messiah, the Choosen One to his people in fulfilment of his promise made long before. (Is 61: 1-3) 'Today, in your very hearing this text has come true.' Thus, Christ Jesus becomes the bridge between the old order and the new, the Law of Moses and the new commandments which God would send. (Mt 22: 37-39 and Jn 15: 12-13) As he, the anointed One, begins to walk the path of his destiny, so he becomes the bridge, the pathway of our own: 'I am the way; I am the truth and I am life.' (Jn 14: 6) It is a time of expectancy, of hope but, as would happen later on Palm Sunday, it is exhilaration touched with sadness. Encompassed within this beginning is portentous reference to the events which would bring about his life's end. For Jesus' rejection by those people with whom he had grown up in close community is the heralding of his ultimate rejection, which would end in his crucifixion.

However, Jesus does not allow his awareness of the events of the future to influence him adversely. He does not allow the rejection by his townspeople to affect his moving forward into a ministry of teaching and healing. When we move forward in our lives into new situations, we can sometimes be hampered by what has happened in our past, or by rejection of the moment. Sometimes moving into new spheres can cause rejection by those who have been close to us but who do not understand that we need to change our situation in order to grow and develop. This can be very difficult as people with whom we have shared close friendships might no longer wish to do so, not being able to understand that what might have been suitable for us previously is now no longer the best thing. This can be particularly the case when we take Christ fully into our lives for the first time. Those around us may not see the need or importance for us in so doing. They may try to dissuade us from continuing our lives with a different emphasis from before, wishing us to remain as we were. However, if this is the case we should try to be strong and know that fully committing ourselves to Christ can be only beneficial to us in the long term, even if it can perhaps cause some initial difficulties. We should look to Christ Jesus himself for the example he gave us in Nazareth.

Secondly, we can often hinder our growth and development as human beings, as children of God, by our desire to cling on to old memories, old habits, old ways of being and behaving. We make it difficult for ourselves to form new ones, instead of putting the past in its rightful place and using what we have experienced in it to guide us in the future, both learning by our mistakes and consciously continuing its positive aspects and developing them. We must remember that the future can be dictated or influenced by what we do, feel or think today. So, today, the here and now, the present is the time to take up our chances, make use of opportunities, and move forward in optimism, open to all possibilities, instead of dwelling in the past or day-dreaming about the future. And let us be sure that the chance to grow in closer relationship with Christ Jesus is one of those opportunities that we take up today.

O Lord, touch my heart, that I may feel,
touch my soul that I may receive your Spirit.

Sunday

I am he: I am the first, I am the last also. With my own hands I founded the earth, with my right hand I formed the expanse of the sky; when I summoned them, they sprang at once into being. (Is 48: 12-13)

Readings: Gen 1: 1-31 and 2: 1-3

We do, as human beings with human minds, have a tendency to try to explain God, to understand him, to rationalise what or who he is. In order to try to move closer to him, we first seem to need to give to ourselves and each other a firm explanation of him, one that our minds can take hold of satisfactorily. Our finite, physical minds seem to have a need to encapsulate him within the limits of our earthly understanding. We can then feel secure and safe.

This need on our part to feel safe and comfortable with complex phenomena manifests itself regularly as we carefully compartmentalise our knowledge and belief, as we explain cause and effect in a logical manner, and as we contain our concepts and experience within boundaries. It seems that we are not able to cope or to expand our awareness if something occurs which does not fit into the accepted patterns of our human existence.

Children, when they are growing and developing, need boundaries to contain them to give them security, but boundaries which are loose and flexible enough to be extended outwards and further on outwards as the children develop in awareness. It is quite understandable that even when we are older we still feel the need for certain boundaries within which to operate, in order that we may feel a comfortable measure of security in our lives. However, we should beware of trying to contain God within boundaries which are inflexible and rigid rather than extendable. We can never know God whilst we are in these physical bodies with human minds. A finite being can never fully know an infinite one. We all have our concepts of what God is or might be, and we busily rationalise him and his existence. But he is far beyond our concepts, far beyond our wildest dreams.

As our experience in the world grows and awareness of it and its workings develops, so should our awareness of God. But not in terms of 'explaining' him, rather 'exploring' him, being open to his presence and his possibilities within and without our known

I AM THE ALPHA AND THE OMEGA

world. For nothing is standing still, and at the heart of this movement and growth is God. He irradiates our world with his Spirit; everything holds him within itself and is held by him. He is in every particle, every cell, every atom. There is nothing in the world that he does not infuse with his loving Spirit. The concept is breathtaking. Likewise is the thought that our planet, our world, is one of many, one of innumerable 'heavenly bodies', the evidence of which we see on dark starlit nights. Look up at the stars and contemplate the vastness of God, for each of these stars contains him and is contained within him, is irradiated by and infused with his loving Spirit. Contemplate, then, both the vastness and the minuteness of God – and be in awe.

For it is easy just to think of God as the intimate Father, close within us, concerned for our well-being and welfare, involved in our every move, caring in detail for each of us and for every other part of his created world to the minutest degree. 'Are not sparrows five for twopence? And yet not one of them is overlooked by God! More than that even the hairs on your head have all been counted!' (Lk 12: 6-7) We forget that the loving Creator, who is so closely concerned with each of us, was and is also he who said: 'I alone, I made the earth and created man upon it: I, with my own hands, stretched out the heavens and caused all their host to shine.' (Is 45: 12) He it is who is creating, upholding, irradiating and infusing continuously. He may not just be continuously developing and extending us and the rest of his created world through his irradiating presence, but may also be continuously extending and expressing himself, becoming greater than already utter perfection.

Our minds cannot conceive of limitless creation, unlimited perfection, infinite expression – how then can we dream of trying to 'know' God with our minds? Rather 'know' him with our hearts.

To you, O Lord, who spread your creating arms to the stars, to you who hold the infinite universe in the hollow of your hand, in awe, I come.

Monday

Who is he, this King of glory? The Lord Almighty – he is the King of glory. (Ps 24:10)

Reading: Ps 29: 1-4

'Who is he, this King of glory' and where is his kingdom manifest? He is our Lord God, our Sustainer, our Creative Source from which sprang the universe in all its manifestations and which is still upheld by him. And where shall we look for his kingdom – in his created world, all around us and within us. Let us explore his vastness and minuteness, his power and his delicacy, his majesty and his awesomeness.

'The God of glory thunders: the voice of the Lord echoes over the waters,' – stand beside a great waterfall and be attuned to the force of the water as it hurls itself over the precipice; feel the power of God, the presence of God within it. Even with a small waterfall can this be felt, but consider the power of God present within the volume of the Niagara Falls: 'the Lord is over the mighty waters.'

'The voice of the Lord is power,' – stand and watch a thunderstorm rolling across the sky. See and hear the power of God within it. 'The voice of the Lord is majesty,' – listen to a stirring piece of music and be attuned to the essence of God within it. Remember that it is only an echo of the music of the heavenly realms. Listen to the silence when it has ended and feel the presence of God powerful within the stillness.

'Ascribe to the Lord, you gods, ascribe to the Lord glory and might,' – go outside and experience a sunset. Be aware of the intensity and variation of its colours, as it spreads over the expanse of the horizon, hosting in its centre the blazing ball of red. Absorb the experience; take it into your being.

'Ascribe to the Lord the glory due to his name;' – look closely at mountains and rock formations; look at pictures of the Grand Canyon or, if you have the opportunity, visit it yourself. Stand in awe at the variety of shape and pattern of the rock structure, as if an infinite imagination had come into play when it was formed. Wonder at the fact that Leonardo da Vinci, when carrying out his studies of the human heart, saw within its caverns similarities between those contained within the rock structures of the natural

I AM THE ALPHA AND THE OMEGA

world. The mysterious rocks depicted in one of his famous paintings are thought not to be rocks at all but representations of the structure of the heart. Consider the Infinite Being who could bring about similarities in structure of areas so vast and areas so small, formed of vastly different material and with vastly different properties and purpose, yet so similar in shape and pattern.

'Bow down to the Lord in the splendour of holiness,' – and lastly consider the perfection of a minute flying insect, no bigger than a pinhead, with all parts particular to an insect complete, right down to diaphanous wings a fraction the size of the pinhead-sized body. There is almost more wonder in the perfection of a tiny insect than in the grandeur of the Niagara Falls.

In the face of all these phenomena in our natural world, who else could be the King of glory but their Creator and Sustainer – our Lord and God?

O Lord, thou art my God: I will exalt thee, I will praise thy name; for thou hast done wonderful things.

Tuesday

For the Lord God is a sun and shield; the Lord bestows favour and honour; no good thing does he withold from those whose walk is blameless. O Lord Almighty, blessed is the man who trusts in you. (Ps 84: 11-12)

Reading: Ps 19: 1-6

'For the Lord God is a sun,' – if we consider our dependence upon the sun for our life on this planet we will understand the significance of the psalmist's image. Sunlight nourishes plant life and we are in turn nourished by plants, directly and indirectly. All living organisms in fact depend indirectly upon sunlight. It keeps in motion the growth and development of plants and we need this continuous process in order to exist. Plants need energy from sunlight in order that the process of photosynthesis might take place through which they make their food, and ultimately release oxygen into the air. We are thus dependent upon plant life for both our food and oxygen, and without sunlight plants could not survive. So the light from the sun is essential for our existence on this earth.

Likewise consider the states of darkness and light. It would be almost impossible for us to live continuously in darkness. We need the light of the sun for our own healthy growth and development. We also need the balance of light and darkness for harmonious living, so that we might have times of waking and sleeping, of activity and rest. So the movement of the earth around the sun each day also brings us balance and harmony: 'His rising is at one end of the heavens, his circuit touches their farthest ends; and nothing is hidden from his heat.' It is not surprising, then, that ancient man worshipped the sun as giver of life and bringer of harmony and balance.

So through the finely balanced and ordered food-chain, God provides our physical bodies with the earthly nourishment that they need. At the same time, through his presence working within each of us on a higher level, he provides the sustenance necessary for our spiritual well-being. However, although we are made easily aware by the demands of our physical bodies of the kind of nutrients that they need, and are visibly aware of lack of them, how many of us are totally aware of our spiritual needs and lack of fulfilment of these? How many of us are aware that by not being open and receptive to the presence of God within us we are starving ourselves of spiritual food essential for our true well-being? We may feel that we are looking after ourselves by nourishing our bodies and minds, but are we also nourishing our souls? Are we letting God the Sun shine into our spiritual lives, warming and expanding and encouraging our growth on this level? For without attention to our soul life we cannot be truly whole and healthy. We will become out of balance, disharmonious, in the fullest sense of the words, even though it may not be obvious in our day to day lives. It is like a plant grown in poor conditions. It grows and develops, flowers and fruits but is a mere shadow of what it could be, given the correct conditions and nutrition. We will grow and develop as human beings but will not really achieve our full potential as spiritual beings, as children of God.

Being conscious of God's presence within us, giving ourselves time and opportunity to spend in his presence, even if only for a few minutes at a time, can begin to give us the spiritual nourishment that we need. It can give us the moments of rest and quietness that many of us need in our busy, full lives, like the time of the day when the sun sets. Or it can give us times of inspiration and intuitive awareness like the moments of sunrise, or recharging of energy and vitality as with the fullness of the sun in the mid part of the day. Whatever our need, we have a constant source of supply and fulfilment if we but look for it, if we go inside ourselves and experience the presence of God, the sun shining within.

God is love; and he that dwelleth in love dwelleth in God, and God in him.

Wednesday

The Lord lives, blessed is my rock, high above all is God my rock and safe refuge. (2 Sam 22: 47)

Reading: Ps 18: 1-3

The words of the psalmist sing out his faith in God as the all-encompassing strength in his life. To him he turns in complete assurance in all situations, knowing that God will always be there to guide and sustain him, to lead him through his difficult times, to be the strong, firm foundation in his life from which he can live and move: 'I love thee, O Lord my strength.'

For each of us, God can be and is the strength in our lives. He is always there to turn to in times of need, when we feel unable to cope without support. He is as sound and enduring as the mountains which we see around us. (Ps 121: 1-2) We can come to him at any moment when we need his strength to support us on our way. In times of pressure we can come to him and 'unload' ourselves onto him – anxieties, fears, anger or whatever we feel the need to share – for he can take it. 'Come unto me all you who are heavy laden and I will give you rest.' (Mt 11: 28) The cause of the problem may not go away immediately, but its effect upon us can be lessened because we will have shared it with God and given it to him. We will have moved away from it, even if only temporarily, and in those moments the distancing from it will help in deciding how best to deal with it. Detachment from a problem area will always help to defuse its power over us. In any situation, stressful or otherwise, enormous benefit can be gained by 'withdrawing' our consciousness from the matter in hand and taking it to God.

This might seem acceptable enough to some in connection with the less important matters in our lives – but what of the more difficult times when apparent disaster hits us? Can we believe that God will be supporting us through these times also, these times when we need the most strength and courage? There are many examples when this has been shown to be the case. One such instance is that of the young man, an office worker, who was in his spare time an amateur athlete, a runner. He suffered an accident and lost part of his leg as a result. This, one might expect, would cause the quality of his life to be diminished, or at least that he himself would regard it as being so. However, rather than sinking into negativity about his situation, he allowed God to be the strength, the rock, in his life. He allowed God to work for him positively, and helped himself and God by trying to make the best of his situation. The result is that he has become a respected coach and speaker in the field of handicapped athletics and is also one of the top international handicapped athletes. He says that he is happier in his life as it is now, because it has opened up so many avenues for him. He feels that his life is now much richer than it was before.

So in these situations not only does God provide strength and support for the person concerned but also, very often, turns them into 'rocks' for other people. Many can take courage and hope from the example set by this athlete, and can go on to make the best of their own situations, having him as an example towards whom to look. Many times those who are apparently struck down by disaster or tragedy can come to be of great service, support and encouragement to their fellow human beings. It might be in pioneering new methods of self-help, or in exchanging previous skills for new ones, as with those who move into teaching rather than performing, such as musicians; it might be in bringing the needs of those such as the disabled to public attention – or, it might be in displaying great strength of character and a deep commitment to and love for God whatever the circumstances. Often, those who seem to be the most afflicted can be the ones who display the most beauty, joy and grace – and these are the people to whom we can look as the truest examples of the manifestation of God as 'the rock' in our lives.

In him who is the source of my strength I have strength for everything.

Thursday

God, the High God, is my shield who saves men of honest heart. (Ps 7:10)
Reading: Ps 18: 30-35

When employed in time of battle, a shield, if held firmly in place, will protect the user by deflecting any weapons thrown by the enemy. St Patrick in his 'Breastplate' invoked God the Trinity to be his shield and protector, 'the wisdom of my God to teach, his hand to guide, his shield to ward, the word of God to give me speech, his heavenly host to be my guard.' He surrounded himself with Christ's protecting presence and asked that Christ might be within all the situations, especially negative ones, into which he might come: 'Christ be with me, Christ within me, Christ behind me, Christ before me, Christ to guide me, Christ to win me, Christ to comfort and restore me. Christ above me, Christ beneath me, Christ in quiet, Christ in danger, Christ in hearts of all that love me, Christ in mouth of friend and stranger.'

We, also, can employ this prayer of protection in all circumstances when we experience fear, or prior to moving into any situation in which we expect to do so. These can be times when we might have to take on a potentially difficult or dangerous situation, or simply something which we have to undertake about which we are feeling nervous. To surround ourselves with the love of God in Christ, to ask that we might be completely enfolded in his care and to speak the words of St Patrick's prayer, can have enormously strengthening and reassuring effect upon us. It can be the means of deflecting, like a shield, those feelings of fear or nervousness that assail us. It can help us to feel protected and secure that we will be looked after whatever the eventuality, whatever presents itself for us to deal with. It is the difference between going out to face something difficult on our own, and going out to face it with someone by our side, helping, supporting and encouraging us.

In a different way, God's enfolding love can be seen as a deflector of any negativity sent towards us by another. The effects of this negativity, whatever it be -- bitterness, anger, frustration or aggression – can be eased by love. These feelings may be caused by our own deliberate or accidental thoughts, words or actions, or may be coming from deep unhappiness or frustration within the person concerned about themselves – the person needing, therefore, an outlet. Whichever is the case, love is the best answer. Negativity in the latter case, received with love and understanding, can help the sender of it to come to a realisation about him or herself. In the former case, love can again be the way forward, as we ask in humility for loving forgiveness and understanding of our weaknesses, mistakes or flaws from the person concerned. To ask God to enfold ourselves, those concerned and the whole situation in love and harmony can help to protect us all against further difficulty. Another way in which this can be done is to make a special effort to pray for those who are causing us problems or pain, or those whom we are not able to like, no matter how hard we try. It can be a powerful and effective instrument if we make an effort to take, for example, one whole week and every day within it pray sincerely for these people, asking that God might enfold all of us in his love and lay his healing hand upon the areas of problem.

Lastly, we can regard God's love as the epitome of the love given to a child by its mother. Just as any loving, caring mother will shield her child from danger or difficulty, so God shields us with his all-protecting love. It is a love that is unconditional and all-enveloping – we cannot 'win' it by anything that we say or do. As any caring mother loves her child simply because it is her child, and not for any gifts or attributes which it might possess or display, so God loves each of us, just as we are, with his all-embracing love. Whoever we are, whatever we are, whatever we do and in whatever situation we might find ourselves, we can always trust in his shielding, protecting love.

Keep me like the apple of thine eye; hide me in the shadow of thy wings ...

Friday

God is our refuge and strength, an ever-present help in trouble.' (Ps 46: 1)
Reading: Ps 46: 1-7

How many times do we hear of people who, in moments of crisis, call upon God to help them in their times of distress? How often do we ourselves, in times of trouble, turn to God for his aid and support? And how often we hear of prayers in these situations being answered, God hearing the call for help and sending that which is necessary for the assistance of those people in crisis or in trouble.

Very often we hear reports of those who have been involved in a disaster, or subjected to the horror of a hi-jacking or kidnapping as having said, 'I just kept praying, singing hymns, holding onto God and knowing that he would come to my rescue, help me through the difficult hours until my release.' Or we hear of those cases where, after a crash or an earthquake, people have been trapped for long periods of time, seemingly without much chance of being rescued. Yet, despite this they have with courage and determination, held on to their faith, their firm belief that God would come to their aid. They have asked for help and trusted that their efforts to make themselves heard would lead the rescuers to the area in which they were trapped, finally effecting their rescue. In all these situations they knew that God would not let them down. He heard their call and responded to it, as he has promised to do for us all in times of need: 'For God himself has said, "I will never leave you or desert you;" and so we can take courage and say, "The Lord is my helper, I will not fear;"' (Heb 13: 5-6) Whatever the situation, we have the full assurance that if we call upon God when we are in trouble or distress, he will always hear us and respond to our needs.

However there is another aspect of the idea of God as our refuge and strength that we might explore. Let us consider the idea of the psalmist's 'City of God, which the Most High has made his holy dwelling,' as being like our own inner centre, that part deep inside each of us in which dwells the spark of God's Spirit, his presence within us: 'God is in that city.' Nothing can disrupt this inner place of peace, security and quiet. It is untouchable – 'she will not be overthrown.' We all have this place, this inner sanctuary, this part of our being where we can more closely feel God's presence. It is to this inner centre that we can try to go to commune with God during times of trouble, sorrow or distress: 'and he will help her at the break of day.' By doing this we will open up an avenue for God to pour into us his loving Spirit, to be a salve for our sorrow and distress, and be a support in our trouble.

We may feel that it is too difficult to find this place within us, this sanctuary, but we all have the capacity to find it and use it. It just may take a little practice at first. To help ourselves we could initially visualise a place which we regard as special to us; it might be in a garden, in the countryside, beside the sea, in a church. Then we can imagine ourselves to be at peace within this place, communing with God and feeling his presence all around us. This can now be our 'sanctuary', our special place within ourselves to which we can 'go', that is, imagine ourselves to be, when we need to be at peace with God, and to receive the blessing of his comfort, strength or reassurance. In any situation where we feel troubled, distressed, pressured or upset, we can move into our 'inner sanctuary' to be with God, even if it is just for a few moments. A few moments of withdrawal from whatever is causing our troubled state can be of great help to us.

But, the most important point to remember, to know for certain, is that we are never alone in any situation, whatever it might be. God never leaves us. He is always with us, always upholding us and always infusing us with his life-giving Spirit. He will never let us down – we can rely on that, for he has given us his word.

The eternal God is thy refuge, and underneath are the everlasting arms.

Saturday

I am the root and the offspring of David, and the bright morning star. (Rev 22: 16)

Readings: Num 24: 17 and 2 Pet 1: 16-19

The morning star is the star which shines in the east at dawn, heralding the beginning of the new day. It is the bridge between the night and its stars and the light of day. In this reading Peter refers to Christ Jesus as the morning star. He speaks about Christ Jesus' fulfilment of the prophecies and God's pronouncement that he is his Chosen One. As the morning star is the bridge between night and day, so Christ Jesus is the bridge between the old covenant and the new, the Law of Moses and God's new teachings for his people. He heralds the new day for humanity, the new opportunities we have because of his coming into the world, teaching and living his message of love, peace and harmony. He heralds the beginning of our new life with him in God – the means through which we can be reborn in the Spirit, our resurrection, if we take him fully into ourselves and our lives.

We can ask Christ Jesus to be the morning star in our life as we start each day, for each day is like rebirth. At night we effectively 'die' to our conscious minds and are 'born again' into our consciousness, into the world in the morning. Thus we can regard each day as a new beginning – a time when we can put behind us those things which we did not quite manage to get right in the day or days before; a time when we can reach out and take up the opportunities which present themselves with fresh enthusiasm; a time when we can begin to do those things which we have been putting off, things which might make a noticeable difference to our lives or to someone else's. Let us allow our morning star, Christ within us, to shine into a visit to a sick person, writing a long-delayed letter, a helping hand to someone who needs it, a time of quiet to be with God, reading a chapter of a book which might give us food for thought.

Let us make each day into a fresh start where we try to put old ways of thinking or behaving, which we know to be now no longer relevant, behind us. We can ask Christ Jesus to be the bridge between yesterday and today, to be the solace and counsellor of the day before and the inspiration and hope for the one ahead. Let us ask Christ Jesus, our morning star, to shine into all that we do, all our daily tasks especially the mundane ones, and transform them into gifts which we can rejoice in giving to God. Instead of grumbling about our work or home routines which we may feel to be dull or boring, we can make them into a living prayer where we joyously dedicate them to God, being thankful for the health in body and mind which gives us the ability to carry them out. Even if we feel tired or not so well at the start of the day, more especially in these cases in fact, we can still try to focus on Christ Jesus, asking him to give us the strength and healing which we will need to take us through the day ahead. We can return to this whenever we need to as the day proceeds, thanking him in anticipation of his help.

As we move on into the day, we can be strongly aware of the presence of Christ at our mealtimes, extending our consciousness across the country to all those who might, at the same time, also be sharing a meal, and giving thanks for this. We can extend it across the world, experiencing fellowship with those in different countries, or different nationalities, and feeling the sense of oneness in Christ that this can bring. We can take our awareness to the time of sharing experienced by Christ Jesus and his disciples at the Last Supper, bringing ourselves into union with them, then and now, as Christ Jesus joins us all together within himself. We can remember those who at their mealtimes may not have as much as we have to eat, and we can, in the days to follow, make some provision for their assistance.

For the morning star in the sky shines on us all alike, wherever we are, whatever we do and whatever our particular circumstances. As this morning star shines upon us all, so Christ Jesus, our morning star, shines within all our hearts, treating us all as equals, loving us, each one in the same manner, and having compassion and understanding for all of us whatever our situation and circumstance.

Arise, O morning star, arise, and shine within our hearts.

Sunday

I am the Light of the world: whoever follows me will never walk in darkness, but will have the light of life. (Jn 8:12)
Reading: Jn 8: 12-19

How difficult it is to be in almost total darkness and to have to feel our way around in it. However, when someone walks before us shining a lantern or a torch, how much easier it all becomes. Christ Jesus presents himself to us as this shining lantern, offering to light our way and assuring us that once he has become our guiding light we will never again be left in the darkness, the darkness of unknowing, the darkness of doubt and uncertainty, the darkness of obscurity. He seeks to enlighten our hearts and minds; to tell us of our potential as children of God; to show us our spiritual possibilities and to lead us towards developing them; to teach us the mysteries of the inner kingdom, the kingdom of heaven within us. Once we have embraced him, listened to his words and teachings, followed his compassionate example, we can never again be in darkness, in a state of unawareness.

In accepting Christ Jesus into our lives we bring into them a constant source of illumination and the potential for enlightenment. He has given us his spoken word to learn from and absorb, (e.g. Mt 5). He has given us the example of his way of life for us to follow. And he has given us guidelines to help us develop awareness: of ourselves and our spirituality, of our fellow human beings and theirs, and of the possibilities of our growing relationship with God. (Jn 14: 15-21) Christ Jesus is the constant, ever present reference point for us in all our various situations. He is the pathway to wisdom as opposed to knowledge, offering us the 'light of life' rather than being lost 'in darkness', the darkness of ignorance. He is the clear, bright light leading us forward, showing us which way to go on our path when we are in doubt. Lastly, Christ Jesus is our accompanist through life, giving a richness and a deeper quality to it in the same way that an accompanist brings enhancement to the performance of the musician, singer or dancer with whom he or she is working.

Consider an illuminated manuscript and the way in which the beauty of the writing and the words is enhanced by the visual decoration. The words may give us the basic meaning but the colour and adornment increase their impact upon us. In the same way, we may, as children of God, have inherent qualities of goodness but the infusion of the Spirit of Christ within us enhances our capacity for such qualities, increases our spiritual awareness, and enriches the quality of our spiritual lives.

In a similar way, think of a stained glass window. The colours and arrangement of the various pieces of glass form beautiful pictures or patterns. However, on a dull day, although the colours and shapes are still visible, they are not shown to their best effect. Now consider the difference when the sun comes out and shines through them. The true nature of their colour and patterning becomes apparent and their beauty is fully revealed – thus they need light behind them to be fully appreciated and to be seen at their best. We are like these stained glass windows. When we work from our own volition we can display our various 'colours and shapes', our abilities and gifts, our strengths and our good points. However, when we allow Christ within us to shine through, how much more apparent these become. Christ will kindle the spark of God, the essential good dwelling within us, just as the sunlight filters through the window bringing its colours to life. He will irradiate this spark, enhancing its power just as the sunlight falling strongly on the windows causes them to glow with intrinsic radiance. And he will fan the spark into a living flame which irradiates us and all with whom we have contact, just as the sun, shining fully through the glass, throws down onto the surrounding area shafts of glowing colour.

So let us allow Christ Jesus to be the light on the pathway, illuminating our inner selves and guiding us in our lives. Let us allow him to irradiate us with his love and truth so that it turns us into glowing stained glass windows; and let us allow him to kindle the flame of God living within us so that we will never again 'walk in darkness'.

The flame of love is a continuous outpouring of life
for those who shine it forth.

Monday

The people who walked in darkness have seen a great light: light has dawned upon them, dwellers in a land as dark as death. (Is 9:2)

Readings: Is 9: 2-4 and Mt 4: 16

Isaiah heralds the dawn of a new era, the birth of the Messiah, he who will bring light to illuminate the world, the light of a new inner awareness, the light of a new consciousness of the self as an individual and a moving away from a collective patriarchal consciousness, stultified by ancestral tradition. For 'the people who walked in darkness' had become stultified by their traditions, those which reached right back to their forebears. They were still trying to live in a collective patriarchal consciousness, believing that laws and rules laid down by Moses were still, in their original form, applicable to them in their present lifetime. Their society had moved forward and developed but the Law had not moved forward along with it.

Customs, beliefs, social structures change and vary as new ideas, new possibilities are explored and experienced, sometimes discarded and sometimes retained. It is healthy for this to happen or else society becomes stagnant and jaded. It needs an influx of new life, new waves of thought and experience periodically in order to stay wholesome. However, the Jews were trying to 'live in the past', caging themselves in 'in darkness ... in a land as dark as death' – in traditions no longer relevant. Christ Jesus tried to demonstrate to them the need to move forward into new more fitting social patterns and belief systems.

Christ Jesus asks each of us to be open at all times to fresh possibilities, fresh directions in which we, as individuals, as social groupings and as society as a whole, can move forward. There are always in society areas which need reviewing, rejuvenating and improving so that there can be more conscious awareness of and provision for the needs of different groupings of people. For example, there should be regular reviews of areas such as housing, health care, prison conditions and aftercare, the care of geriatrics and the terminally ill. We are each responsible for ensuring that for ourselves as individuals and for society as a whole, the quality of life maintained is of the highest standard.

I AM THE LIGHT OF THE WORLD

We each have a voice which can be used in this context, in innumerable ways. We could remain mute saying to ourselves, 'What can I do about this? I am only one person so I can have no effect on this situation.' But every voice counts, every person's opinion, idea, or feeling matters. We can write letters of support and agreement or dissatisfaction; we can make a telephone call; we can attend a public debate – in order that an awareness of our feelings and those of others may be brought to the higher echelons of our social hierarchies – our M.P., our County Council, our Personnel Manager. On a different level we can participate in community schemes – neighbourhood watch, care for the elderly or disabled, holiday playschemes for children, rota schemes for visiting the sick or solitary. Within our church there are prayer groups, prayer 'chains' where people link with each other on a list, prayer boards, voluntary visiting, support groups – the list is endless. The key words here are personal involvement and social responsibility.

We should not be afraid to launch out and explore new possibilities for social responsibility in our lives. It will enrich our experience of life and deepen our social and spiritual awareness as a result. It is important to try to review our present precepts, beliefs and opinions constantly and keep our minds open and receptive, instead of remaining stagnant in our own fixed ideas, opinions and experience, our own personal little pools of darkness. 'Lord, that I may seek to console, rather than to be consoled; to understand, rather than to be understood; to love rather than to be loved. For it is in ... self-forgetfulness that we find our true selves.' (*St Francis*)

As the glorious golden-red light of dawn dispels the darkness, may the light of Christ illumine our minds, bringing to them greater awareness. With the rising of the sun the land is suffused with warmth and light, causing all living things to expand and unfold. So may the love of Christ irradiate our hearts so that they expand into openness and receptivity and unfold into an outpouring of warmth, concern and compassion for all.

May our darkness be dispelled by his great light and may his shining breath bring warmth into our hearts and souls, granting us strength for action in peace with all people.

Tuesday

The light shines in the darkness, and the darkness has not overcome it. (Jn 1:5)

Reading: Jn 1:1-14

'The real light which enlightens every man was even then coming into the world.' Some thought to try to put out the light but the light was not extinguished. Instead it burned more strongly, entering into many smaller lamps and kindling the sparks within them. So that in the place of one strong light shone many smaller ones, each fed within by the light. Thus the light spread all over the world illuminating many of the dark areas, and continues to do so.

Light will always conquer darkness. If, in an area of total darkness a match is struck, even though it may only give a minute amount of light, the effect of the all-consuming blackness is negated. If the match then lights a candle, this throws out a pool of light dispelling a still larger area of the darkness. When Christ came into the world to bring us the light, the light of love and truth, he did so in order that we might take it into ourselves and shine it forth, as the candle shines forth the pool of light. We must live and move from the centre of light, of love, within ourselves. Everything we do from this centre can contribute to the spreading of love and healing in the world, to conquer the darkness. Without each of us playing our part there can be little hope of the healing of the world's problems. For there is still a great deal of inhumanity, injustice and cruelty in the world. There is much ignorance and blocked awareness. We see pain inflicted by some people upon others, upon God's creation and upon the planet earth itself. We read about innocent victims tortured, mutilated or murdered. We hear of unfair trials ending in execution; unfair imprisonment; the taking of hostages and the holding of them for bargaining power; the killing of innocent people. We may feel useless or ineffectual when we hear of these things, wondering what, if anything, we can do. Christ's charge to us to love one another must be the starting point for our efforts. 'I may speak in tongues of men or of angels, but if I am without love, I am a sounding gong or a clanging cymbal.' (1 Cor 13:1) If just one of us works through love we become like the candle enlightening the surrounding dark atmo-

I AM THE LIGHT OF THE WORLD

sphere. A hundred lighted candles will give many times more light and heat than one. So if a hundred of us work from the centre of love within ourselves, the area of love and healing in the world will become many times greater and more 'darkness' can be transformed.

Each loving thought, each act of love and compassion, each loving prayer is seen and known by God and those working with him. Christ and his ministering angels can take our thoughts, our prayers and our loving actions – our individual and collective points of light – and spread them across the world to illuminate those of us who are still spiritually in darkness. What is needed for those who inflict cruelty, pain and injustice on others is an awakening of their higher, true natures, a realisation of the spark of God within them. Then an understanding of what is good, true and just can be brought into their conscious awareness. We can help by sending thoughts of love to them, by asking and visualising in prayer that they may be completely surrounded and enfolded in God's love. Through the power and compassion of Christ working within them, and the ministering of his angels to them, we may assist with our prayers in his awakening of their true higher selves and in his opening of their hearts to love rather than hate, cruelty or inhumanity. We all need to play our part in this. Enfolding a person, place or situation in prayerful love is one of the strongest things we can do – it can have enormously beneficial effects. It has been said many times that negative situations did not get out of hand but were contained at a bearable level by the power of loving prayer – many potentially inflammatory situations have been eased. Also many situations have ended in a positive vein the initial stages of which promised quite the reverse.

Prayer is the powerful medium by which we can assist Christ in spreading the light through the world and if, through prayer, all the 'candles' can at last be lit, then the whole of the darkness will be transformed.

Everything, when once the light has shown it up,
is illumined,
and everything thus illumined is all light. (Eph 5:13)

Wednesday

And in their presence he was transfigured; his face shone like the sun, and his clothes became white as the light. (Mt 17:2)

Reading: Mt 17: 1-8

The disciples, Peter, James and John, were privileged to share in a special moment with Jesus when he, in the company of Elijah and Moses, was transfigured in their presence. Here they had proof of who he really was. They saw him radiating and being irradiated by the Spirit of God: 'his face shone like the sun, and his clothes became white as the light' in the company of two spiritual beings come down from God's presence. When Peter saw them conversing, he wished to capture and preserve the moment, but the moment passed with the overlighting of Jesus by the Holy Spirit and the disappearance of Moses and Elijah.

When we have times of spiritual uplift, deep peace or happiness, great enjoyment or fun, we are inclined, like Peter, to want to cling on to those moments, to keep ourselves in that state for as long as possible and not let those moments go. We would like to encapsulate ourselves in the precious moment, make time stand still so that we do not have to leave it and continue with our normal everyday lives. Of course, this is not possible. If we read on we find that while Peter, James and John were absorbing a profound spiritual experience, the rest of the disciples were struggling to heal a boy suffering from epileptic fits. They were unable to deal with the situation, having to wait until Jesus returned for him to cure the boy. So while some were experiencing spiritual uplift, others were struggling with physical need and difficulty. Time, therefore, could not be held still for there was an outside world clamouring for attention and help. This is the case with ourselves. We cannot cut ourselves off and experience perpetual spiritual bliss while there is work to be done in the world around us.

Christ Jesus had his times of profound communion with God but he did not dwell in them. He went forth from them into the world to work harder teaching, preaching, and healing the sick and needy. To have remained on top of the mountain, transfigured, with Moses and Elijah would not have been fulfilling his life's purpose.

I AM THE LIGHT OF THE WORLD

We all have a responsibility both to God and to ourselves to do the same. However, this is not to deny ourselves the times of uplift, peace or joy, for without them we would find it difficult to carry on in life. Instead of clinging on to them, wanting to capture and preserve them, we should regard them as times of inspiration and hope from which we can move forward in greater enthusiasm and courage. We can bask in the afterglow, using it for nourishment and self-expansion. In times of difficulty or apparently insoluble problems, we can then bring back into our mind and being, the feelings experienced in those moments of peace or upliftment. In times of sorrow we can, in our minds, turn back to those times of joy and contentment that we have had in our lives, and we can use them to ease the sadness that we are experiencing. We can take reassurance from them at times when we think God is no longer near us, knowing that he has allowed us the privilege of participating in these special moments which we can treasure in our hearts.

For often these moments are not of our own making. We can attempt to create a profound spiritual atmosphere or situation where we experience great joy, peace or happiness. Yet often these moments come when least expected – an impromtu gathering of friends, an unplanned visit or letter from a friend, a very moving prayer time where we felt the presence of God very closely, a profound communion service, a breathtaking vista on a country walk or drive, the full arc of a deeply coloured rainbow. These, for me, are examples of God's grace, moments when he touches us, his children and his earth, with his loving hand and bestows upon us a precious gift for our enjoyment or inspiration. May we always be conscious of and grateful for the gifts from his treasurehouse.

I will sing the story of thy love, O Lord, for ever.

Thursday

While I am in the world I am the light of the world. (Jn 9:5)

Reading: Jn 9: 1-12

In this passage Jesus gives sight to a blind man. 'He was born blind so that God's power might be displayed in curing him.' Here we see Jesus heal physical blindness. But blindness can also exist on an inner level and here also has Christ Jesus offered us healing and wholeness. (Jn 12: 46 and Rev 3: 20) Inner blindness can be the result of rigid and inflexible beliefs, opinions and perceptions, through which we become blinkered, unable to see God's truth and the workings of his Holy Spirit. We are unable to see situations from another's viewpoint, from different angles. We cannot adapt to new ideas, fresh possibilities. We become 'blocked in' and unseeing. So how can we begin, through Christ Jesus, to heal this inner blindness and to find the enlightenment and fluidity of awareness that he offers?

We need to come to a deeper understanding of ourselves – an awareness that certain areas need to be examined and developed, modified or healed. We tend to battle on, pushing aside our inner needs or fears and ignoring those darker inner spaces which we do not acknowledge or fully understand. The 'sore places' from painful past experiences become internalised and blocked in causing negative personality patterns. Perhaps we have been let down in business or in relationship. 'I will never trust anyone like that again.' It is better that the pain and problem is brought out after a time and looked at closely in God's loving company and in that of a trusted friend or priest or counsellor. It can then be seen for what it is and through loving counselling or comforting, helpful words, in God's loving presence it can be healed.

How else can we seek to open up and understand ourselves more fully? We can spend some time each day in reading and reflection. If we could lay aside just a short time for this and be disciplined in carrying it out, it could become an essential and enriching part of our daily lives. Much wisdom has been given to us by those past and present such as St Francis, Julian of Norwich, Jean-Pierre de Caussade and others nearer our present experience. The bookshops, particularly Christian ones, are full of books relating people's experiences of God, of suffering, of working in deprived communities, of healing and wholeness. There are many to choose from and each that is read brings another dimension to our own experience of life as we share the author's experiences, thoughts, feelings. We may see parallels in our own lives and areas from which we may learn. Add to this a daily reading of God's word to us and we will be given much 'food for thought' upon which to reflect.

However, there is another way, a way still more important, and that is being in communion with God as much as possible. If we allow him space and time each day, he can and will reveal many things to us, things which can lead to a greater understanding of ourselves and others. Each morning, sitting quietly for a few minutes, relaxing both mind and body, we can try to clear away any thoughts, and just focus on God. If distractions come in we can let them drift away again. It may be helpful in focussing on God to visualise a beautiful painting of Christ, or to repeat a sentence of prayer or a hymn, or simply repeat the word God or Christ to ourselves, whatever comes naturally. Then we can imagine his spirit filling us with love and peace. If there is something which troubles us or causes us concern in our lives, we can offer it to him; or if there are aspects of ourselves which are troublesome or blocking us in some way, ask that he will work on them with us in those moments which we spend together. We can ask him to stay with us throughout the day, guiding our actions and words, thoughts and feelings so that whatever comes our way we will know that he is with us and that we are not alone. From this we can develop inner strength, inner security and inner awareness. Thus our developing relationship with God and his supreme and all encompassing love for us will help to heal our 'inner blindness' so that in time we can come to a greater understanding of self and others through an expansion of our consciousness.

Loving Spirit of God, gather us in to you
that we may come to know you, and thus ourselves,
more fully.

Friday

You are a light for all the world. (Mt 5:14)
Reading: Mt 5: 14-16

It is a common saying, 'Do not hide your light under a bushel,' spoken to those who do not use the particular gifts or talents that they have. We are all better at some things than others or have specific gifts that we may or may not use in our day to day lives. But how many of us recognise this and use them to the full? If we do not we can be like the servant who, when his master gave him one 'talent', a coin, took it and buried it in the ground. The other servants did something productive with theirs, but this servant did not want to take the risk of losing what he had been given and so preferred to bury it. (Mt 25:14-30)

If we, like the servant, bury our talents we might be denying something to our fellow human beings. Consider the scientist, going about his work as a representative for a scientific firm, who was called by God to become ordained a priest. If he had remained where he was many would have been deprived of his resultant profound and sincere ministry. Instead he responded to God's call and became a 'beacon of light' bringing much help, wisdom and joy to innumerable people. He did not hide his light under a bushel, he let it blaze forth into the world and many people were warmed, illuminated and guided by it.

So this man chose to allow Christ to shine through him, showing him the path that God wished him to travel. We may feel that we do not have a special skill or gift – we cannot all be great painters, musicians or political figures. However, our particular gift may be that we are good listeners or have a sympathetic nature, to whom people feel they can safely come and tell their troubles. Many shop assistants and bar staff are using their special gift when they greet their customers with a warm, friendly smile and exchange feelings about life or work. Regular customers can feel that there is someone who is interested in them and will take the time to chat to them. What a joy it must be for those who live alone, elderly perhaps, who can look forward to a warm greeting and a chat with a smiling shop assistant. These people are shining as 'beacons of light' although they probably do not realise it. Many a time a warm smile has brightened up a miserable day for someone.

I AM THE LIGHT OF THE WORLD

So there are many ways in which we can be 'lights for all the world'; a thoughtful gift, well chosen, for a friend; a hoped-for toy for a child; a much-needed kind word spoken at the right time; a helping hand offered – the list is endless. Not only on these occasions do we become beacons of light shining out but we generate a reciprocal response in the receiver and thus allow them to be the same. Who cannot be moved when they see the eyes of a child light up in response to a birthday cake with candles lit. They are enrapt with the appreciation of a joyous experience. Their eyes shine and their whole being seems to be illuminated. Through their joy, their light, we are given the chance to shine with pleasure too. But children have the gift of experiencing a pleasurable moment in the depths of their whole being, a gift which most of us seem to lose as we move away from our childhood. They experience the totality of life within themselves. We, on the other hand, realise that we are all part of the totality of life and need to be in relationship with God and with each other to be fulfilled.

So, if we invite Christ into our hearts and our lives and ask him to light us up with his love, we can shed that light and love amongst our fellow human beings. Then will we each be able to make God's love manifest in our lives and in the fulfilment of our relationship with each other.

Stay with me, and then I shall begin to shine as thou shinest, so to shine as to be light to others.

Saturday

And the city had no need of sun or moon to shine upon it; for the glory of God gave it light, and its lamp was the Lamb. (Rev 21:23)

Reading: Rev 21: 22-27; 22: 1-5

Here we are given a glimpse of a perfect world, the holy city, the new Jerusalem – a place of light and truth, goodness and beauty, joy and plenty. It is paradise on earth, all who dwell there being in complete union with God. 'They shall see him face to face, and bear his name on their foreheads.' This is God's ideal for us, his children. We are also given, at the beginning of the Bible (Gen 1,2), another paradise, another place where heaven touches earth but there is considerable difference between the two. This paradise is newly formed, fresh and innocent, but also unaware, unconscious and naïve. Adam and Eve, humankind, are not yet ready to experience conscious spiritual awareness. However, in John's description of the holy city, we are given a picture, a glimpse of an enlightened paradise, one whose inhabitants have a conscious awareness of God and live in his presence; they shall see him face to face. Adam and Eve had no experience of life to bring to their paradise but these people have a wealth of human experience, both individual and collective which they have brought back to their Creator.

A good teacher gives out his knowledge and inspiration to his pupils and students. He opens up and shares himself with them, his feelings and thoughts on various subjects. He offers his experiences to them for them to learn by. Each one of his pupils or students takes what has been given and uses it however best it suits them to do so. They may choose to discard it but most will take it and benefit from it, allowing it to enrich their awareness, stimulate their interest and imagination, help them in their growth and development. The teacher will see how they have taken and developed what he has given them in the following months or years that they are together. In future years he may hear of how it has been used on a long-term basis and be joyful that seeds sown by him reaped a good harvest.

In a similar way we have all come from God to grow and develop as individual beings, to experience and explore as fully as we can this human life and to grow and develop in our spiritual life. Just

I AM THE LIGHT OF THE WORLD

as the teacher is enriched by the outcome of his work with his pupils and students, so we can bring back to God the products of our experience so that he may glory in them as the fruits of his children, we to whom he has given life and being. He gives us a picture of ourselves in the state of ultimate union with him, empowered and illumined by his Spirit, 'nor will they need the light of lamp or sun, for the Lord God will give them light ...', and desires the best for us, his beloved children, as does any good parent.

'And its lamp was the Lamb ...', and the means by which we can move towards this vision of bliss, of paradise, is 'the Lamb', Christ Jesus, he who has given himself as mediator, as signpost, as guide, as pathway. He it is who can enable us, can help us to develop on our spiritual path. He can shine on the roadway in front of us, guiding us and showing which way to go, by which means to learn and grow in our lives, both spiritual and earthly. If we open ourselves up to his presence within us we need nothing more to empower, enable and sustain us spiritually. He can be our complete fulfilment if we choose to accept him.

Consider a large central lighted candle, burning brightly. An infinite number of small candles can be lit from it without any lessening of its power and light – whilst burning, it is an unlimited source of both. God in Christ is our inextinguishable flame, our inexhaustable source from which we, as an infinite number of small candles, can be lighted, each shining out in all directions and radiating the love of Christ within us.

For with thee is the fountain of life,
and in thy light we are bathed with light. (Ps 36:9)

Sunday

The Lord is my shepherd – I shall not want. (Ps 23)

Reading: Ps 23 and Ps 80: 1-3

The Lord is my shepherd; I shall not want – in him I am provided for every need in all aspects of my life.

He maketh me to lie down in green pastures – by giving me life, he brings me the wealth and richness of human experience.

He leadeth me beside the still waters – I experience the beauty of true peace and the calm of inner stillness that close communion with him brings.

He restoreth my soul – my spirit is constantly nourished and renewed through his presence within me.

He leadeth me in the paths of righteousness for his name's sake – he constantly opens my awareness to what is true and right and good in my life; through Christ Jesus showing me the way, he reveals to me his teachings of the inner kingdom, the kingdom of heaven.

Yea, though I walk through the valley of the shadow of death – many times may I feel threatened by situations, overshadowed by depressive thoughts and negative feelings, overwhelmed by feelings, tasks and responsibilities, blocked in or stultified by weaknesses and inadequacies.

I will fear no evil: for thou art with me – yet, I will not give up; I will not 'cave in' under external pressure; I will not sink into hopelessness, for I can feel your presence constantly within me, loving, sustaining and upholding me in whatever inner state or outer situation I may be in.

Thy rod and thy staff they comfort me – I am always protected and guarded from harm by your presence as long as I am open to your loving Spirit; I can always find solace for my aching heart in your arms of love and can enfold myself and all my 'hurting' places within you.

Thou preparest a table before me in the presence of my enemies – I find all that I need for my journey through life and the adversities I experience when I come to your table, come into your presence to be nourished and fortified.

I AM THE GOOD SHEPHERD

Thou anointest my head with oil; my cup runneth over – you cover me with grace and blessing; your ever-living Spirit fills me constantly with love and sustenance so that it pours out from me towards all others.

Surely goodness and mercy shall follow me all the days of my life – my inner and outer lives are greatly enriched by your abiding presence, your constant inflowing and out-pouring of love and goodness.

And I will dwell in the house of the Lord for ever – and I will live and move and have my being always enfolded within you.

Loving Shepherd, through your goodness we shall want for nothing;
in your presence nothing shall harm us;
nothing shall separate us from your loving arms.

Monday

'I am the good shepherd; the good shepherd lays down his life for the sheep.'
(Jn 10:11)

Reading: Jn 10: 10-13

In this passage Jesus shows us the difference between a hired sheep 'minder' and a shepherd. The hired minder is just doing a job. When he comes up against a problem or dangerous situation he just leaves and runs away from it. He lacks commitment. For him the sheep are just part of the 'deal', to be watched over but in themselves worth little or nothing. In any situation it is more important for him to save his own skin than theirs. For the shepherd, however, it is quite different. The sheep are his charges, objects of his love and care. He is willing to face and surmount any difficulty or danger in order that none of them might be harmed. He is committed to caring for them.

In calling himself the Good Shepherd, Christ Jesus is showing his commitment to us. 'I am the good shepherd,' committed to loving and caring for each of his sheep individually and the flock as a whole. 'The good shepherd lays down his life for the sheep' – committed enough to be self-sacrificing for the sake of those in his care. And Christ Jesus made the ultimate self-sacrifice, giving up his earthly life that we all might have the opportunity to have eternal oneness with God. He demonstrated the lengths to which he was prepared to go that we might have access to greater spiritual development. He showed us by example what it means to be a good shepherd.

What can we learn by this? Can we follow his example in our own lives? It often seems to take major disasters for humanity to bring out these qualities in itself. Here, many times we see mothers sacrificing their own needs for those of their children, often nourishing their children as best they can to the detriment of their own health. Again, at times such as floods or serious crashes, children are often handed over to the rescuers first so that they may have the highest chance of survival. And, too, on other occasions, people will sacrifice their own chances of survival to help others to live, as in one tragedy at sea when one man formed a bridge with his own body over which others scrambled to safety. On all these occasions people were displaying the qualities of the shep-

I AM THE GOOD SHEPHERD

herd. They were showing real commitment to and concern for the welfare of those whom they loved, those in their care and their fellow human beings in general.

But we need to show our commitment to Christ and to each other in our everyday life. We may feel that we do so already but there can be many weak areas such as: fear – of being let down, taken advantage of or hurt, for to love and give of oneself to another is to make oneself vulnerable; and laziness – it being easier to keep ourselves aloof with only peripheral involvement with others. But Christ wants us to be committed to him and to one another in love. 'Love one another; as I have loved you, so you are to love one another.' (Jn 13:34) He does not pretend that it will be easy. In any relationship with each other there must be give and take, which often requires much love and understanding. In taking on the needs or demands of another person there must be willingness in certain situations to sacrifice one's own comforts or desires for their sake or for their happiness, and this requires commitment. For Christ showed us that his commitment was far reaching. Amongst those for whom he died were the ones who betrayed, condemned and crucified him. There could not be greater commitment than that. Yet he understands our weaknesses and shows us that his commitment was made not just once with the ending of his earthly life on the cross, but continuously as he offers himself to all of us whenever we want to be close to him or to receive help, healing or guidance from him – 'for everyone who asks receives, he who seeks finds, and to him who knocks, the door will be opened.' (Mt 7:8) We just have to accept his offer.

You have chosen and called us, Lord, to be your family.
Your name, your essence, is pure love.

Tuesday
I am the good shepherd – I know my own sheep. (Jn 10:14)
Reading: Jn 10: 14-18

Every dedicated shepherd knows his sheep. To some or even all of them he might give names, sparked by some idiosyncracy, some quirk in their behaviour. The shepherd knows their habits and particular ways, what to expect of them. He knows if they are weak and prone to disease or if they are vigorous and strong. Each is recognised as an individual. The sheep, also, in time become accustomed to their shepherd and there will develop between them a certain rapport.

Christ Jesus offers himself to us as the good shepherd – he who knows his sheep individually. He tells us that our relationship with him can potentially be as close as that of himself and his Father. Christ Jesus closely experienced the presence of his Father – the complete understanding and all encompassing love; the richness of the working of God within him: '... as the Father knows me and I know the Father ...' As he and his Father were one, so he is at one with us. Christ in God knows, understands and loves us all completely. He knows each of us intimately – our particular ways and idiosyncracies, our strengths and weaknesses, our potential. He has a complete understanding of each of us: ' I know my own sheep and my sheep know me ...'

The opportunity is always there for us to develop the rapport of the sheep with the shepherd. Christ Jesus has given us the offer to be in close communion with him whenever we choose to be. (Jn 14:23) He knows each of us intimately; he calls us by name. Do we hear him? He knocks at the door to come into our lives. 'Behold, I stand at the door and knock: if any man hear my voice, and open the door, I will come in to him, and will sup with him, and he with me.' (Rev 3:20) Do we open the door and let him come in?

For we know when he is calling, when he is speaking to us, when he is urging us to come and be close to him. We hear that quiet but persistant little voice that keeps speaking to us in our mind and heart. Often we push it away into the background. We do not want to listen because we are too busy or preoccupied to be attentive or to respond. Sometimes the words being spoken do not fit in with what we want to do, or we are too tired to make the effort to hear what is being said. Sometimes we do not want to hear words which we know to be true concerning the way we have behaved in a certain situation. Perhaps we feel that it might be easier to live our lives away from the promptings of the quiet voice, to block it out altogether and just to operate on a certain level where we live only for fulfilment of our sense awareness. Yet, the voice comes from love, the wide and profound love that Christ Jesus feels for each of us. If we feel that there is concern in it, or faint reproval even, we cannot feel rebellious towards it, for the voice of our own conscience only says the same thing if we allow it the space to do so. And to operate on the level of our five senses alone is to deny ourselves the richness and depth of a fulfilling and joyful spiritual life which, in the long term, is far more rewarding than temporal pleasures.

Those who live to experience the sense 'pleasures of the moment' alone can be likened to 'the other sheep of mine, not belonging to this fold' – not yet fully aware of the quiet inner voice – 'whom I must bring in; and they too will listen to my voice.' We must, by example and by openness of spirit, help others to a closer awareness of the presence of Christ Jesus within them – but only after we have fully 'opened the door' for him to come into ourselves.

Fear not, for I have redeemed thee:
I have called thee by name, thou art mine.

Wednesday

My own sheep listen to my voice. (Jn 10:27)
Reading: Jn 10: 22-30

Good shepherds can inspire the trust, confidence and respect of their charges through compassionate leadership, encouragement and understanding, as can good teachers and good managers. Christ Jesus taught and led his followers by example. (v. 26) In offering himself to us as the Good Shepherd, he makes himself available to those who wish to follow him as a living example of his own teachings, a personification of the positive attributes of a shepherd, teacher and leader. (v. 27) While we have our minds and our hearts focussed on him, we cannot in a spiritual sense be harmed: 'no one shall snatch them from my care.'

It is, however, easy to be affected by the constant distractions of our daily lives. We can be bombarded by conflicting ideas, contradictions, temptations. Our lower natures can be affected by the media: visual 'conditioning' can exaggerate greed or possessiveness if we are prone to these things. We see beguiling advertisements for this and that and somehow develop an overwhelming need or desire for things in our lives that up until now we have managed without quite comfortably. We are bombarded by pictures and descriptions of the 'latest' everything and feel we must have them. We can also become greedy for knowledge – we must buy this or that book, attend this or that course and possess the knowledge that they contain or present. We become greedy for wisdom. However, we cannot buy wisdom or attain it through greed or possessiveness.

Wisdom comes from being linked with our creative Source and communing with him. It means sitting quietly attuning to him, listening to the 'still, small voice' within each of us. We can try to find him in the 'fires, earthquakes and strong winds' of an exciting, stimulating lifestyle, but we, as Elijah experienced, will find him best in the 'still, small voice'. (1 Kings 19: 11-14) Christ Jesus did not lead a 'racy' life, full of external stimulus to find fulfilment. He shows us by example that a wealth of accumulated worldly things, material or experiential, is not necessary for true fulfilment. (Lk 12: 13-34)

I AM THE GOOD SHEPHERD

However, sitting communing with God is only part of the way to attain wisdom for we are social creatures and are all one in God, so we should not isolate ourselves completely. It means moving out into the world, not for self-gratification but with a deep awareness of God within us. In this way we can participate in whatever comes before us, with an awareness of Christ working in us and in those with whom we come into contact. We must move from the knowledge that we are enfolded by him at all times and keep hold of that awareness. We must take from each experience that from which it is possible to learn, to grow and to develop.

However, sometimes we can feel confused, not knowing the right way to go, what is true and good in a situation, what is the moral or ethical action to take. In all of this we need to keep a strong awareness of Christ Jesus' teachings and actions. We can test the water of the situation by considering how Christ Jesus would have dealt with it, how he would have acted, what his likely response would have been. We have as a yardstick, always, the description of his life and work in the gospels and the knowledge that in all situations he moved and acted from love and compassion, never from selfish motives. If we find ourselves besieged by conflicting feelings and thoughts about circumstances or situations, we may feel that in all the conglomeration of visual, mental and emotional stimuli we are liable, at any moment, to slip out of God's caring arms and drown in a mass of confusion. However, Christ Jesus has assured us that we are all at one with him (v. 27), and that provided that we hold on to him in faith and trust at all times, 'no one can snatch them out of the Father's care.' We are his, for always, once we have made our commitment to him and have allowed him to come into our lives. He will never leave us in whatever situation we find ourselves or however confusing and conflicting the circumstances: 'I give them eternal life and they shall never perish.' We just need, in our hearts and minds, to keep holding firmly onto him.

Thou wilt keep him in perfect peace whose mind is stayed on thee.

Thursday

I am the door of the sheepfold. (Jn 10:7)
Reading: Jn 10: 1-9

One definition of door or doorway is 'means of access'. Christ Jesus offers himself as 'the door', the means of access to and from the 'sheepfold', a close union with God. He assures us safety and 'pasturage', God's loving enfoldment and spiritual nourishment if we stay united with him. In this way we can live and move in the world from a firm, secure foundation. (v. 9)

However, Christ Jesus warns of those who try to enter the sheepfold by other ways. Some try to attain it by the merits of their own egos. But they can be deceiving both themselves and those whom they try to influence. They may be seeking to achieve spiritual upliftment but are going about it in the wrong way. It is easy to think we know best and to go ahead of Christ rather than follow him, laying out the path to our own specifications. It is easy to tell God what we want and go out to try to get it instead of listening to what he wants for us. Instead it requires humility, as Christ Jesus showed us, not egotism.

It is also easy to be beguiled by false gods. There is the god of social esteem – over-attentiveness to praise and flattery can inflate both our heads and our egos. We begin to put ourselves on a level with God instead of remembering that we are receptacles for his Spirit. We can become too self-important by the reliance of others upon ourselves, and we can begin to feel completely indispensible rather than acknowledge the working of God within us. Many times has someone been over-loaded because of failure to delegate, thinking themselves the only person who can deal adequately with all the situations on hand. Often a heart attack or another stress-related illness is the consequence necessitating the withdrawal of the person concerned, and yet the company, committee, or whatever it is, still continues to function quite adequately with someone else in his place.

Then there is the god of social standing which allows one to climb the social, political, or career ladders with no regard or compassion for others, any who are in the way being carelessly or even ruthlessly disposed of.

There is the god of affluence which can beguilingly turn a healthy concern for one's welfare and enjoyment of life into greed for excess and a false need for more and more material possessions – this, when there are others in great need in the world. Lastly, there is the god of laziness or irresponsibility which can cause negligence in the consideration of one's duty as a human being to others.

There are also the 'false prophets', persuading or beguiling us to follow courses of action other than those which we know intuitively to be right and true. Many of us can get into situations in which we do not want to be, or do things which we know are not right, simply because the rest of the group want to do it and we cannot face being the odd one out, or ridiculed as 'chicken' or 'goody-goody'. There are also those who seek to persuade us to go against our better judgement for their own ends – they may need a scapegoat or an accomplice in some action they wish to take. Christ Jesus warns us of these: 'Beware of false prophets, men who come to you dressed up as sheep while underneath they are savage wolves. You will recognise them by the fruits they bear.' (Mt 7: 15-16)

In all these cases and situations, we must keep ourselves firmly fixed on Christ, ask that we might be held and enfolded in his love, and follow his voice, that inner voice by which he leads us now, showing us which way to go and reminding us of our responsibilities. We can and will recognise the voice of truth and goodness within us and we must be brave and strong enough to follow its dictates. 'When he has brought them all out, he goes ahead and the sheep follow because they know his voice.'

Come, my way, my truth, my life: such a way as gives us breath,
Such a truth as ends all strife, such a life as killeth death.

Friday

Rejoice with me ... I have found my lost sheep. (Lk 15:6)
Reading: Lk 15: 3-7

The strong feeling from this passage is the deep love of the shepherd for each of his charges, and the extent to which he is prepared to go to ensure that each one of us is kept safely close to him. If one strays away from the rest, he is prepared to go searching until he has found it, after first ensuring the safety of the others. Christ Jesus shows us that the love of God for each of us, our welfare and our well-being, is that of the perfect shepherd. 'I myself will tend my flock ... I will search for the lost, recover the straggler, bandage the hurt, strengthen the sick, leave the healthy and strong to play, and give them their proper food.' (Ezek 34: 15-16) What a warm and tender picture these words give us.

How much like these sheep can we be seen to be. We can 'straggle' in the distractions and uncertainties of ephemeral pleasures and satisfaction, unwilling to search for and experience deeper meaning in our lives. We can lose our way in the mire of deliberate wrongdoing, harmful both to ourselves and others, or accidentally, weakly be led away by others from what we know to be right and true. We all make mistakes at times, some of us more than others. We all err in our thoughts and actions. There are many stones on our path over which we may trip and fall down. But each time we do, we must try to pick ourselves up, dust ourselves down and continue. If it is too hard to do this by ourselves, we have only to look around us and there we will find an outstretched hand, always there to lift us up and help us on our way – and sometimes to carry us when things get too tough. 'But I have noticed that during the most troublesome times in my life there is only one set of footprints. I don't understand why when I needed you the most you would leave me? The Lord replied: My precious, precious child, I love you and would never leave you. During your times of trial and suffering, when you see only one set of footprints, it was then that I carried you.' *(Footprints in the Sand)*

Whenever we fall down on our path or stray from it, Christ Jesus will always come looking for us to bring us back into close union with him. There are many ways in which he comes searching: in the meeting up with someone, by chance or otherwise, who can

I AM THE GOOD SHEPHERD

give us help or advice; in words spoken by someone we trust at just the right moment, (like golden apples in silver settings are words spoken at the right time. Prov 25:11); in something pertinent to our situation read in a book; in a look or gesture of kindness given when we feel 'in the depths', with little faith left in ourselves or in humanity; in seeing someone worse off than ourselves; in actions or words of another which strike a chord in our conscience or inner being; in a sight which might touch our heart. Christ Jesus not only whispers in our inner ear but also works through his people.

It is important to realise and accept that none of us is perfect; we all lose our way from time to time and need rescuing. There is something else worth remembering when we are feeling bad about our 'unforgivable' thoughts or actions and consider ourselves worthless in God's eyes: that is, that often it is those who have made the greatest errors whom God calls to work strongly for him. Or those who have realised their mistakes and have moved away from them in genuine sorrow and sincerity. Consider St Paul who, having spent years persecuting Christians, received a vision of Christ Jesus in which he was asked why he was persecuting him, Christ Jesus. (Acts 9) He went on to become one of Christ's greatest advocates. Also consider the woman who came to Jesus to anoint his feet; she had moved away from her true path but had come in sincerity to express her love for him. When he was criticised for having allowed her to anoint him, he replied: '... her sins, which are many, are forgiven; for she loved much ... Thy faith has saved thee; go in peace.' (Lk 7: 47-50)

We should hold on to the knowledge that no mistake is irredeemable, no experience wasted, even if it is a negative one. It is all part of our experience of being human and living in a human world. If we feel guilt because of what we have done, we have the assurance that, if we are truly sorry, God will always forgive us. (Lk 15: 11-32) He accepts us for the imperfect beings that we are. He will always come to our 'rescue' and will rejoice that we have returned to him. Then will we be able to leave the error or wrongdoing behind and move forward in faith to new beginnings.

Amazing Grace! How sweet the sound that saved a wretch like me.
I once was lost but now I'm found, was blind, but now I see.

Saturday
Simon, son of John, do you love me? ... Feed my sheep.' (Jn 21:17)
Reading: Jn 21: 1-17

Peter felt hurt that Jesus seemed to need confirmation of his love for and dedication to him. He felt that Jesus doubted him and that his faith was being brought into question. Yet each time his faith was tested, he was given a new task by Jesus: 'feed my lambs' – nourish my young followers and nurture their nascent belief; 'tend my sheep' – care for my older followers, strengthen and sustain them; 'feed my sheep' – develop and extend the faith of these followers with your teaching and example. Jesus was asking Peter to make a firm statement of his faith and his commitment in order to entrust to him the continuation of his work.

Each time we try to follow Jesus' example, or to speak of him and his teaching to others, we are making a statement of our own faith. If we are to make such statements we need to be sure that they are rooted in a firm foundation. If we are to be messengers of Jesus, representatives of his teaching and love, we cannot afford to be half-hearted in our own faith. This would not be doing justice to him. In order to follow Peter and 'feed my sheep' we need first to make our firm and clear declaration: 'Lord, you know everything, you know I love you.' We need to truly believe that in whatever situation we are doing Christ's bidding, he is supporting us and filling us with his love.

But our lives at times can be full of doubt and weakness. Does God really love and care for us as much as Christ Jesus says he does? Do we really know for sure that he is there with us always; that we have a spark of him within us, our inner reserve of love and life that we can enter at will at any moment to strengthen and sustain us? It can often feel quite frightening to move out into certain situations where we know that our faith will be tested. Sometimes when we try to speak of Christ Jesus and to live according to his way, we can face rejection, ridicule and antagonism. It requires courage to stand up for what we believe to be true and right in the face of derision or criticism. In these situations we need to hold fast to the knowledge that Christ does really love us and that we will never be rejected by him, even if we are by some of our fellow human beings. If we could move in our lives from a true and full

I AM THE GOOD SHEPHERD

awareness of his love, it would not matter if we are rejected or scorned by some of those with whom we have contact. For love can, like water, flow around obstacles. If we can look past the rejections and see Christ in the other person, we will realise that the rejection comes only from the level of the personality. It may be the result of problems or blocks in the person concerned or in ourselves. There may be reasons why we are not compatible. But this does not necessitate our reacting in a negative manner. It might be giving us the chance to see something in ourselves that needs to be overcome or changed or developed along a different route, and similarly within the other person. If we hold on to Christ and stay in communion with him, he will be able to help us to transform our 'difficult area.' Or if we try to look for Christ working in the other person and continue to send them love and prayer they may gradually move into a greater awareness of themselves and their own 'difficult areas,' there is much evidence of relationships or situations between people being changed through prayer.

If we could just forget ourselves, our doubts, insecurities and self-centredness and set our hearts and minds on Christ, looking for him in both ourselves and in those whom we meet, we could be free from many of the fears which hold us back in our interaction with others.

So, can we strengthen our faith by setting our hearts and minds on him so that he can work in and through us? If we can, we will in time reach the point where we are able to give him, in complete trust, all of ourselves and our lives – and not count the cost.

To give and not to count the cost ... and to ask for no reward save that of knowing that we do thy will.

Sunday

I am the true vine, and my Father is the gardener. (Jn 15:1)
Reading: Jn 15: 1-4

Every good gardener knows the value of pruning, cutting away old plant growth in order that new growth may appear or that new shoots can grow out more strongly from main stems or branches: new growth, if the old is taking all the goodness from the main plant; new shoots, if old growth means that the plant will out-grow itself and become thin and straggling. Bushes such as roses are pruned so that maximum nourishment goes into the season's crop of blooms. Pruning, carefully carried out, is beneficial to the plant, keeping it in better physical shape and allowing it maximum flowering capacity.

In a similar way God can be seen as our 'gardener'. He is both our source of nourishment (v. 4) and our 'pruner': 'every barren branch of mine he cuts away; and every fruiting branch he cleans, to make it more fruitful still.' We, in essence, were created in his own 'image and likeness.' (Gen 1:26) However, the essence of each of us is overlaid by many things, including the limitations of living in a physical world. The brightness of our true inner selves tends to be clouded over by the demands and machinations of our physical selves. God's plan is for us to be strong, healthy, 'plants', 'fruitful branches,' reflections of himself in all his love, truth and goodness. We can, at some point during our lives, become like the 'barren branch', having some dead wood, some unnecessary psychological or emotional 'rubbish' which needs clearing away. Or we can become like the plant which grows too quickly towards the sunlight, overshooting itself and becoming thin and straggling – rushing forward in the hasty acquisition of knowledge and experience without having sufficiently 'digested' previous experience. We therefore do not have a firm foundation of life from which to move forward, leaving us, perhaps, rather immature. We can become cluttered by too many beliefs, ideas, opinions and concepts, so that strength and conviction is taken away from our real 'belief system', our faith in God.

We can have too many commitments, too many 'irons in the fire', so that our energy is so diffused that we do not give a proper amount of time and energy to commitments of major priority, thereby producing many sub-standard blooms instead of two or three strong, beautiful ones. In all these cases we need a good 'gardener' to keep us in shape, to trim off 'dead wood', to nourish our 'roots', our foundations in faith and in human experience. When we open ourselves to God and invite him to work with us in our inner and outer lives, we give him opportunity to clear away the dross, to refine us so that we may become the kind of people that he wants us to be, reflections in our physical lives of our inner, essential selves, reflections of his presence within us.

For there will be areas of our lives which we may have to come to terms with, parts of ourselves which may have to be faced and changed, and sometimes it may not be a very happy experience. It is never very pleasant to come face to face with our shadow side, that side of us which we want to try to forget about, the side of ourselves which we turn away from and do not want to own or to acknowledge. Yet, in order to be 'more fruitful still', this often has to be done. We will already have been partially 'cleansed' or refined by Christ Jesus' call to us and our decision to follow him. (v. 3) Let us go all the way, give ourselves completely to our 'gardener' and let him prune and transform us such that we become the 'fruiting branches', the 'perfect blooms' that he wishes us to be.

By his grace he can make us as like him in inward being as we are in outward form. This is his blessed will.

Monday

I am the vine, and you are the branches. He who dwells in me, as I dwell in him, bears much fruit; for apart from me you can do nothing. (Jn 15:5)

Reading: Jn 15: 5-10

In this passage Christ Jesus likens himself to a vine giving us an example by which we can understand how God's living Spirit upholds and sustains us, through the medium of Christ himself. The vine plant springs up from the earth – Christ comes forth from God. The plant is nourished and sustained by the nutrients in the earth – Christ is empowered by God's Spirit. The plant puts out shoots which grow into branches upon which, in time, grow and ripen its fruits, nourished from the nutrients flowing up from the earth through the central stem. Christ Jesus, the vine, is the central stem springing from the Source and channelling nourishment to these branches, ourselves. Through him we were each given more opportunity for individuation. The branches are individuals, all part of the whole plant and sustained by the same source, yet each is a separate entity producing its own leaves, flowers and fruit. Without Christ living with us, taking on the human aspect of creation and crossing the barrier of death back into the spiritual realm we would not have had the opportunity of self-realisation and self-development that his gift and sacrifice brought.

Christ opened up the possibility for us to individuate within God's loving care, developing in our own particular way towards him and experiencing our own personal spiritual reality. He gave us the capacity to come to God, the great Source of all things, as individual parts of him with individual experience and consciousness – to be gathered up together as one great whole in the fullness of time. So we are all branches who, if we continue to be joined with Christ, can grow and flower 'bearing fruit in plenty'. In this way we can experience 'the Father's glory' – the fulfilment of his desire to express himself completely through each one of us, and thereby we can enter the great joy of close communion with him.

Christ is the vine itself, the main plant from which we individual branches spiral out. A plant carries within it the essence of all its off-shoots – stems, flowers, fruit. Christ Jesus, as the perfect human being, carries all of us within him. The apostles each had his own quality for which he was chosen. There were twelve apostles;

twelve different personalities, twelve different potentials to be developed, twelve different expressions of God. Christ Jesus, as the thirteenth, was also the One, the entirety, the complete whole, containing all of their qualities within himself. We each have our own individual gifts, qualities and potential. As was the case with the apostles, Christ contains all of these. He, as the perfect and complete human being, encompasses all our potential, all our possibilities. We are, each one and all, contained within him.

Branches, however, if cut away from the plant, wither and die through being deprived of their nourishment. If we are branches, we cannot expect to move away from Christ and still be sustained in the same way as when joined to him. We end up like withered branches collected up and burnt. It is not to say that the Spirit of God would not still be active within us, giving us life, for he is in everyone and everything at all times. But our quality of life would deteriorate. We would experience great emptiness, lack of spiritual vitality, lessening of spiritual awareness. We need him, just as he wants to be, within us. We need his all-encompassing love to sustain that in our hearts, our inner centres, fanning the spark of God's love that dwells in each of us. He says: 'Dwell in my love'– be aware of his presence within you, the availability of his love, his help and understanding; move towards an awareness that we are indivisibly connected with him if we choose so to be. 'For ... neither death, nor life, nor angels, nor principalities ... shall be able to separate us from the love of God, which is in Christ Jesus our Lord.' (Rom 8:38-39) If we follow his teachings and his example, if we keep ourselves joined to him in love and trust, then 'He who dwells in me, as I dwell in him, bears much fruit.'

Branches of the tree are many, but the tree it is just one;
Petals of the lotus are many, but the lotus is just one;
And I love you, Lord.

Tuesday

The kingdom of heaven is like a mustard seed, which a man took and planted in his field. (Mt 13:31)

Reading: Mt 13: 31-32

If we look at a tiny seed lying in our hand, it is almost impossible to imagine that if we plant it in the soil, in a few months it will have become a strong flowering plant. A few mixed handfuls of seeds can, within a relatively short time, have become a colourful, fragrant flowerbed, hosting a wealth of insect life. The mustard seed in the reading grew big enough to hold roosting birds. What potential, therefore, is contained within the handful of seeds, what possibilities it holds, how much sustenance it can give to a host of other creatures.

One manifestation of the kingdom of heaven in us could be seen as the seeds that God has sown within each of us, our potential as his children, which, with nurturing can grow into a beautiful 'flowerbed'. We can each be seen as 'gardens' for God. God has laid out the plan: the capacity for much beauty – loving thoughts; much fragrance – loving words; and much vitality – loving actions towards others. He has given us our respective gifts and talents by which those with whom we have contact can benefit, as did the insects and birds from the flowers and tree.

We can add to what God has already planted in our 'gardens'. We can sow thoughts of love, positivity and thankfulness there and nurture them into strong 'plants'. Loving, compassionate thoughts both generate love within ourselves and love radiating out to others. 'Like attracts like' – those who give out warmth and love can receive warmth and love in return. However, it may not necessarily be returned by the person to whom it is given. Many times can one carry out an act of kindness and generosity to someone for no expected reward, and within a space of time find that one has received in return something of a comparable nature, often in unexpected circumstances. It appears that the more positive, loving thoughts one has, the more that seems to generate similar responses in one's daily living. So we can sow seeds of love and kindness in ourselves and keep nurturing them by affirming what we are doing. That is, when negative thoughts come in we can try to remember positivity and love and transform them where pos-

I AM THE TRUE VINE

sible. This is not necessarily easy, especially if one has a tendency to let one's thoughts go in a downward spiral, which many of us do. However, if we find our thoughts slipping into negative mode, if we are feeling 'low', or if the situation we find ourselves in is depressing, we can try to think of something positive in our lives or in the world, something to be thankful for, something to be glad about. Even in the worst circumstances we can usually find something, however small, to be positive about.

For every positive thought a seed is sown which will grow into a beautiful flower, and for every negative one a seed is sown which will grow into a weed. If we have too many of the latter, our 'gardens' will become choked with pessimism and our optimism will be pushed out of the way. So, filling our minds with pessimistic thoughts will generate an air of negativity around us which is not helpful to our flow of love and our interaction with others. It is always uplifting to share in the companionship of a cheerful, optimistic person; more so than with a gloomy, pessimistic one!

There will, of course always be times for each of us when we cannot help feeling 'down'. We might have difficult circumstances, unhappy news etc., and it is quite understandable to be miserable in these situations. But in day to day living, when times are not too difficult, we can try to be more conscious of transforming our negative thoughts, our little niggles and complaints about ourselves, the world and others, into a more positive vein. It really can make a big difference in our lives if we try hard to look on the bright side of things; it can generate a more positive atmosphere all round, for ourselves and those who share in our lives. Let us therefore sow thoughts of love, understanding and optimism in our 'gardens', that they might increase and spread into both our own lives and into those with whom we come in contact.

Ever living Lord, keep us always close to you,
that we may grow in the ways that you have planned for us.

Wednesday

The kingdom of heaven is like yeast, which a woman took and mixed with half a hundredweight of flour till it was all leavened. (Mt 13:33)

Reading: Mk 4: 26-29

If you have ever watched a loaf of bread being made, or made one yourself, you will know that an essential ingredient is the yeast. You will have noticed that after a while the dough will begin to rise, although the workings of the yeast are imperceptible. It is a subtle and gradual but highly effective process. Similarly with the sprouting seed in the story from St Mark's gospel. The man who planted it does not know how it sprouts and grows.

God's Spirit in the world, his love in action seems sometimes to move as imperceptibly as yeast, as mysteriously as the sprouting seed. 'God moves in a mysterious way, his wonders to perform.' There are situations which have been in deadlock for a number of years and seem to have no solution. It seems that there is no means of finding one, or removing the cause of the problem or deadlock. Yet, somehow, after a time the unexpected can take place – a situation breaks and there is the opportunity for moving positively forward, or a solution is found. It may be where in a country dominated by a repressive regime or dictatorship which seems immovable, events move fast and unexpectedly bringing about the liberation of its people. It may be when someone in prison suddenly is able to open up and take Christ into him or herself, which results in their his or her life becoming transformed, as from that time.

Lastly, it may be a situation where hostages or prisoners of conscience have been held in captivity for a number of years with seemingly little hope of release. Then, somehow, events move unexpectedly and within a matter of weeks they are freed. This is how the kingdom of heaven can operate in the world – quietly working within people and situations just as the life force works in the seed, unseen and mysteriously. It can bring about in people's lives or in situations a positive transformation, just as the seed is transformed by the life force and develops into a flowering and fruiting plant.

It is fruitless for us to try to work out how and why these changes or transformations take place, for we would need to explain God and that is not possible. However there are ways and means by which he uses us, his people, to bring these unexpected events about. One is by means of the quiet word, the gentle suggestion, the positive, loving example. It is often when someone has shared a thought or suggestion and then left it to work unobtrusively like the leaven or yeast that the person with whom they have left it comes to an awareness of God in Christ within themselves. This can be far more effective than a heavy bombardment of thoughts or suggestions. Often the 'softly, softly' approach works better than a more heavy-handed one, whereby people might feel that they are being dictated to and forced into something that they are not yet sure about.

Another example of the workings of the kingdom of heaven in the world is through the power of faith. (Mt 17:20) In the situation of the release of hostages or prisoners of conscience, often they and those working for their release have held on firmly in faith knowing that in time, God would move events so that their release would be made possible. Often afterwards, they have talked of their faith which kept them going during their hours of darkness. Likewise, those working for their release, their families and friends, the negotiators, have spoken of never giving up hope and keeping faith in their eventual freedom. Faith can move mountains, as a small amount of yeast can leaven a whole loaf of bread. The power of faith is limitless.

Let us not, therefore, underestimate the power of the kingdom of heaven, the power of the Spirit of God working in the world. Let us never give up hope in any situation. Instead let us have faith that, even though it is not visible or obvious to us, within every situation God is working and moving as imperceptibly as the yeast in the bread, and as mysteriously as the life force in the seed.

Rest in stillness within God's love
and let him guide the future as he has the past,
so that, in the fullness of time,
all now a mystery will be revealed.

Thursday

Still other seed fell on good soil. It came up and yielded a crop, a hundred times more than was sown.' (Lk 8:8)

Reading: Lk 8: 4-15

'A sower went out to sow his seed. And he sowed...' Creation was not an event that happened just once, it is happening all the time. God continuously creates within his world, within each of us as his creations. He continuously pours into us love, inspiration, possibilities for goodness and truth, for development and growth. He is, in one aspect, the infinite and universal source of thought and creative ideas from which ours spring and develop. He is the sower of true and right thoughts, inspiration and ideas; from his impulse comes the flow of creativity in the world. They are pure, true and holy when they are released from their source and flow into the 'soil' of our human consciousness.

Some of these 'thought seeds' fall 'along the footpath', that is onto 'unprepared soil' – that human consciousness which has not yet developed a strong enough awareness of the presence of God within. The seeds are trampled on and the birds eat them – the compassionate feelings towards other people, the creative ideas to increase their well-being and welfare, the thoughts of harmony and love become twisted into thoughts of unkindness, ill intent and exploitation of others. Truth and goodness become distorted into insincerity and wrong doing.

Some seeds fall on 'rock' – those human minds and hearts which are initially responsive, as the loving 'thought seeds' touch a chord of truth which resonates within them. But, after a time, the resonance weakens – 'and after coming up, withered for lack of moisture', and dies away. The self-interested aspect of the mind takes over – self first, self second, self all the time. The chord resonating love and selflessness is forgotten; inspiration and creativity is used for self-benefit alone and not shared amongst many for universal benefit. The 'flowers' which grew from God's 'thought seeds' have withered away and new seeds will need to be sown, as with annuals in our gardens, before anything can take a permanent root.

Some seeds fall 'in among thistles' – into minds and hearts full of triviality and caprice or care and worry, so that they are given no space to develop and grow to maturity. The 'thought seeds' of God flow into the midst of whim and fancy, are considered momentarily and are then rushed out again along with all the others. Or they come into the minds of those weighed down with too many 'worldly cares'. For a few moments, the spirits of those concerned are uplifted, but these are quickly squashed down again by the pessimistic, negative thoughts crowding out these peoples' minds and lives. The 'thought seeds' have no time or opportunity to transform this negative environment into a more positive, optimistic one. They are 'choked' by the 'thistles' of negativity – the people concerned never being satisfied with their lives and wasting their energy on complaining rather than seeking positive, productive ways to improve their lot.

However, some seeds fall into 'good soil' and grow and yield ' a hundredfold.' Some human minds and hearts are open and receptive to the creative thoughts of God, which are received in conscious awareness of the truth. The thoughts develop and flourish bringing wisdom, understanding and compassion to those receiving them. The creative thoughts of God enable and expand the minds of the receivers so that they are able to spread wisdom and compassion wherever they go in the world. Through the expansion of their own conscious awareness they are able to help to bring into being in other people those 'thought seeds' sown in them by God. They thereby facilitate the spreading of universal harmony and the increase of the oneness of the Spirit in the world.

'If you have ears to hear, then hear,' Christ said to his followers, and also is saying to each of us now. He has prepared the 'soil' within us for the sowing of the 'thought seeds' of God, the creative inspirational flow that fills us continuously. Which kind of 'soil' do we have? Is it that of the footpath, that of the rocky ground or that which is choked with weeds? Rather let our 'soil' be 'good soil', let our minds and hearts be open and receptive to God's creative thoughts, that we might play our part in the spreading of harmony in the world as we all work towards oneness in the Spirit.

May the word of the Lord deeply enter our hearts and minds, and bring forth from this seed, the flower of truth.

Friday

You did not choose me: I chose you. I appointed you to go on and bear fruit, fruit that shall last ... (Jn 15:16)

Reading: Jn 15: 11-17

In this passage, Jesus changes the role of the disciples from that of servants to friends. As he is about to leave them, they need now to be more responsible for themselves and not so dependent upon his presence amongst them. They have listened to Jesus' major teachings, have shared in his wisdom, his thoughts and feelings. They now have to move into a new, more independent phase where they work more from their own initiative. He has instructed them as much as he can and it is now up to them to find their way in the world together. 'I appointed you to go on and bear fruit, fruit that shall last.' His time to leave them is getting close so they must now continue his work, the spreading of his Father's love and his Father's word in the world.

What comes to our minds when we think of the words 'friend' or 'friendship'? Love, trust, sharing, loyalty, intimacy, joy, security. A true friend is someone with whom we choose to share – lives, experiences, thoughts, joys, sadnesses. A true friend is someone for whom we feel love and affection and from whom we receive it. We can relax with them and be 'ourselves'. They accept us for who we are 'warts and all' – they know our strengths, our foibles; they know our likes and dislikes. They want the best for us. They cheer us up when we are low in spirits; support us when we are weak or in trouble; rejoice with us in our pleasures and our joy. They are priceless: 'A faithful friend is beyond price; his worth is more than money can buy.' (Eccles 6:15)

The word 'servant', on the other hand, suggests something different. He or she is in a subservient role to his master or mistress; dictated to by them and carrying out their wishes. The master or mistress has authority over the servant, arranging or organising those aspects of his or her life which overlaps with or relates to their own. The master or mistress has responsibility for the servant, for his or her well being, actions and work. The servant has little self-responsibility in his or her position.

So Jesus in naming his disciples, 'friends', is granting them a privilege the privilege of intimate partnership, of acceptance, of affection, of loyalty and trust, of sharing. He charges them to love and care for each other as true friends do, as he has done, their true friend. (Jn 15:12) We believe that we are, with the disciples, included in this role – the role of true friends to Christ Jesus, if we wish to be. If we regard ourselves as 'friends' rather than 'servants' there is a significant change in emphasis. Rather than abdicating responsibility for ourselves and letting Christ Jesus do all the work with and upon us, as our 'Master', we take on a new role with more responsibility. As friends of Christ Jesus we will want the best for him, and that means doing our best for him. But apart from trying to improve ourselves, what does this mean? In St Matthew's gospel Christ Jesus tells us, 'For when I was hungry, you gave me food; when thirsty, you gave me drink; when I was a stranger you took me into your home, when naked you clothed me; when I was ill you came to my help, when in prison you visited me ... anything you did for one of my brothers here, however humble, you did for me. (Mt 25: 35-40) Whenever we offer the hand of true friendship to anyone in the world, whenever we offer someone love, care and compassion, we are offering it to Christ Jesus, for he is in all of us, and we are in him. And it means sharing – sharing with him all the things that we share with our human friends – our thoughts, our enthusiasms and hopes, our affections and our joys. For he says, 'I have spoken thus to you, so that my joy may be in you, and your joy complete.'

A servant serves his or her master out of necessity – that is the nature of his or her position. But a person becomes a friend out of choice. Christ Jesus has chosen us to be his friends. (v. 15-16) Have we chosen him to be ours?

He is quick to clasp us to himself, for we are his joy and his delight, and he is our salvation and our life.

Saturday

But the harvest of the Spirit is love, joy, peace, patience, kindness, goodness, fidelity, gentleness and self-control. (Gal 5:22)

Reading: Gal 5: 22-26; 6: 1-10

Paul's words present for us a picture of our true potential as human beings, what we could achieve were God's Holy Spirit to have a 'free-rein' working within us. Often our 'lower natures' get in the way – the results of the various blocks, patternings and conditionings that are manifest in us due to factors, events and influences in our lives up to date. If we could allow God's Spirit to work in us as he would wish, it is within the capacity of each one of us to realise our true potential and it is our task to come as close as we can to doing this.

We all come from God, our Source of life and the One who sustains us. We have the chance, whilst on earth, to come into closer relationship with him. However, while we are here we have our lower natures to contend with, which are just as much a part of being human as our higher selves and should be accepted as such. These need to be tempered by the workings of the Holy Spirit in each of us – and the Holy Spirit works through love. The way we can keep control of our lower natures is through love – on the one hand, love of ourselves as human beings and therefore part of God's creation, and on the other, acceptance of our failings and frailties as imperfect beings. For how can we 'help one another to carry these heavy loads' unless we learn to love, accept and care for ourselves – 'Look to yourself, each one of you.' If we do not truly love ourselves, we cannot truly love God or our fellow human beings, in the same way as loving only one's family and friends and not all others is not loving in its complete sense. 'If you love all alike, including yourself, you will love them as one person and that person is both God and man.' (Meister Eckhart) We are all part of God and his creation, all interconnected through his Spirit, so to exclude some or to exclude ourselves from this flow of love, is to restrict our capacity to give and receive love.

Jesus said: 'Love thy neighbour as thyself.' (Mt 22:39) Love for one's neighbour and love for oneself are closely intertwined. One could argue that to love oneself is to be selfish. But self-love and selfishness are not the same. A selfish person does not love him-

I AM THE TRUE VINE

self too much but rather not enough. It can be an expression of inner frustration and emptiness, a lack of understanding of himself, a lack of self-respect and inner security. So he seems interested only in satisfying his own needs and desires, with little or no concern for other people. Selfish people may not seem to love others but they are not really loving themselves either, by not understanding or attending to the real needs of their inner selves.

Self-love, however, is different. It is the capacity to see oneself as a precious creation of God, a vessel for his Spirit and part of his beautiful world. It is the capacity to be aware of the self-responsibility and the opportunity for self-development that this brings. Each of us is one of God's gifts. So we should affirm this by being aware of and joyful for the essential true and good qualities which we all possess as part of that gift. As God's created beings we are worthy of love and respect from each other and from ourselves, and we do God an injustice if we do not acknowledge this.

One could argue that all of this would lead to self-opinionation and conceit. But that would be the result of loving ourselves as personalities, thinking 'what a great person I am'. But to love oneself as a personality is quite different from loving oneself as a vessel for God's spirit. This is, on the contrary, a very humbling experience as we realise that God, in all his greatness, has entrusted a part of himself into our personal care. The chalice which holds the wine is reverently cared for as a sacred vessel. We, as sacred vessels, need reverently to care for ourselves – our minds, bodies and souls, for just as we treasure the beautiful, shining cup, so God treasures us – his beautiful, shining chalices. Thus can we look towards the reaping of 'the harvest of the Spirit' in ourselves in the fullness of time.

All my being is nothing but vessel for thee;
May the tale of thy coming be spoken through me.

Sunday

I am the bread of Life. He who comes to me will never go hungry... (Jn 6: 35)

Reading: Jn 6: 22-31

The crowd gathered at Capernaum needed 'proof.' They needed proof of Jesus' authority and a sign or signs that would confirm this. 'What sign can you give us to see, so that we may believe you?' There had already been one sign – the feeding of a few thousand people with a very small quantity of food. Jesus told them that they had not looked beyond the sign to what lay behind it. They were not able to see, to comprehend that Jesus himself and not his miracle was God's sign. They were blinkered by their knowledge of him as Joseph the carpenter's son. (v. 42)

We do, as human beings, seem to have a need for 'proof' or 'signs' at certain points or in certain situations in our lives. It may be when, as children, we need a smile or gesture from our mother as a sign that she loves us. It may be when an employer needs to have a sign that the person applying for his job will prove trustworthy. It may be when we have come to what we feel is a crossroad in our life and need to make the right decision as to which way to go, or the right choice between various alternatives. We need a sign which will show us which way to go or which will help us make our decision. We also need a sign that God has not deserted us when we look around and see what is happening in the world – atrocities perpetrated by some people upon others, disasters such as cyclones, earthquakes where many people suffer injury and hardship – where is the sign in these situations that God is still with us?

For us now, as for the people at Capernaum, Christ Jesus is still our sign. 'He it is upon whom God the Father has set the seal of his authority.' The essence of God is love and Christ Jesus was and is the full manifestation of God's love in human form. He exuded pure love, compassion and care. 'I am that living bread which has come down from heaven' (v. 51) – the pure essence of love that nourishes and sustains us, teaches us wisdom and understanding and shows us our path in life. He works within each of us, the more strongly if we acknowledge his presence. We can see God's sign in the smile on the face of a mother which comes from the love that is in her heart for her child and her child feels this and is secure. The sign for the employer can be the sincerity which he intuitively feels coming from his prospective employee. At the crossroads we can find a sign if we ask for Christ's help. It may come through words spoken by a friend, something seen or read in a book that he has led us to and that 'jumps out' at us, or from a strong feeling inside ourselves that the step we are taking is the right one. In times of disaster or atrocity, when God may seem very far away, there is still a sign that he has not left us – in the response from people wanting to help alleviate the suffering and pain of those afflicted. God works through his people. Often, witnessing pain and suffering in others brings out the best in people, their hearts moved with compassion and love for their fellow human beings and wanting to help them. They are in contact with the spark of God within them and reflect his love, as Christ was the supreme reflection and still is. People are moved by love and compassion to help others, and this is intensified by the power of God's love working within them, increasing their own capacity to love. The sign that God has not deserted us is in their actions.

Christ working in us is our constant sign from God – the sign of his love. He works in us all whether we choose to acknowledge him or not – we have our own free will. But to those who do, he will always be, 'the food that lasts, the food of eternal life,' an ever-present, loving proof that the God who cared for the people in Capernaum still loves and cares for us now and always will.

I saw that all compassion to one's fellow human beings, exercised in love, is a mark of Christ's indwelling.

Monday

The bread that God gives is he who comes down from heaven and brings life to the world. (Jn 6:33)

Reading: Jn 6: 32-45

The people at Capernaum regarded Jesus as a 'miracle man' providing food as if by magic. They had not yet arrived at a true comprehension of what 'food' he was in reality providing for them. He tried to show them that they should see him as the real food that God is providing, their true nourishment. When they ask him to give them this real 'bread', he tells them clearly 'I am the bread of life' - your spiritual nourishment, your true sustenance.

Christ Jesus, then and now, is the visible sign of God's perpetual presence in the world and ourselves, and promise for the future: 'For it is my Father's will that everyone who looks upon the Son and puts his faith in him shall possess eternal life.' Christ is both the sign, the means by which we see God's Spirit working in the world and the 'bread', that which 'brings life to the world', that which quickens it on a spiritual level. He is the living channel between God and ourselves, the channel kept constantly open and vital if we accept him completely into our lives, the 'real bread from heaven'. In so doing we will be constantly sustained and vitalised by God within us flowing through Christ, our 'channel'- 'whoever comes to me shall never be hungry and whoever believes in me shall never be thirsty'

If we fully accept Christ into our lives and open ourselves to him, this will facilitate our coming to God in prayer. For through Christ a channel has been opened for us to be in closer communion with God when we pray; provision has been made through him for a freer bi-directional communication between God and ourselves. For prayer is our living sustenance. It is God's gift to us, access to his presence through Grace, the availability of close communion with him, the means by which his Spirit can move within us. It is not a process initiated and activated by ourselves. It is God's activity within us - the means by which he moves us along the path which he has laid out for us. It is the means by which he shows us which way to go, what our potential is, what we can productively develop in our lives - and what we need to grow away from or discard.

Thus God works within us in our daily lives. But still more important is his activity within our soul life. Julian of Norwich writes that 'prayer makes the soul one with God.' When we spend time in prayer, we consciously try to help ourselves on a mental and physical level, but at the same time we help ourselves on our higher, soul level. Our souls have the opportunity to rest in God's presence, to be nourished and revitalised by his Spirit, and to experience the joy of being in union with him. Julian writes: 'Prayer is the deliberate and persevering action of the soul. It is true and enduring, and full of grace. Prayer fastens the soul to God and makes it one with his will, through the deep inward working of the Holy Spirit.' Just as we give our minds and bodies opportunities in our lives for experience, growth and development, so we also need to give ourselves the opportunity of growth and development in our soul life.

Prayer, therefore, can be seen to be of utmost importance for each of us, and it is vital to our well-being that we try to set aside time for prayer, for being in God's presence, as often as possible, even if it is just for ten minutes each day. We may want to bring situations to him from our daily lives, or take an intercessory role for those whom we know, sick or healthy; we may want to come in thankfulness for something for ourselves or for others. Whatever our purpose in coming, it is of utmost importance to experience within our 'ten minutes', some moments of silence where God's Spirit can work within us on a soul level. We may not be consciously aware of anything happening at all, but it does not matter. For God's Spirit will be working in the unseen to our souls' benefit, enabling its growth and expansion, and bringing it into closer union with himself.

The love that God most high has for our soul is so great that it surpasses understanding.

Tuesday

I am that living bread which has come down from heaven; if anyone eats this bread he shall live for ever. (Jn 6:51)

Reading: Jn 6: 46-51

Jesus, in this reading, makes reference to the time when Moses had led the Israelites out from Egypt into the wilderness and they had no food to eat. God provided them each day with manna to sustain them on their journey. (Ex 16: 2-18) Jesus draws comparisons between the manna with which God nourished their physical bodies in those times and the 'bread' that he is providing now for the people at Capernaum. He points out to the latter that God does always provide sustenance for his people, appropriate to their prevailing needs. He explains to them that the Israelites required physical nourishment but that they themselves require spiritual nourishment and that he himself is the means by which they can receive this: 'I am that living bread which has come down from heaven.'

Christ, as the living bread, the living channel between God and ourselves, offers us a constant supply of spiritual sustenance, a continual means of close communion with God. In coming to God in prayer through himself, Christ offers us the chance to develop and deepen our individual relationship with God, by helping us to share more closely with him. For sharing with God is a very important part of our growth in his Spirit. Just as sharing with a friend or family member enriches our relationship with that person, the same can be said for our relationship with God. It can be said that we do not truly know a person until we have spent time in their company – exchanging thoughts and ideas, sharing joys and sorrows, or participating in events and experiences together. The same can be applied to our 'getting to know' God. It can be argued that God knows everything about us, so why do we need to tell him about things ourselves? Yet, in the same way as a parent 'knows' their child, how much more depth there will be in their inter-relating if the child enjoys coming and sharing him or her self or aspects of his or her life with the parent.

So, even though God does know all about each one of us, our desire to come and open ourselves to him does bring an extra dimension to the relationship. By bringing ourselves, our hopes

I AM THE BREAD OF LIFE

and wishes, and all those things which are dear to our hearts to share together, we can immeasurably deepen our relating with him. For he wants us to get to know him, to feel secure and comfortable in his presence, to share with him intimately as we would with a parent or close friend. He wants us to realise that he can be more to us even than they can, if we want him to be more to us than our closest human relationship; more to us than all of our close human relationships put together. His relationship with us, and ours with him, encompass everything that we could ever need. His is the ultimate relationship; he is our all. Julian of Norwich writes, 'He is our clothing. In his love he wraps and holds us. He enfolds us in love, and he will never let us go.'

We can begin our sharing with God as we wake up each morning, speaking with him and feeling his presence within and around us, asking that he might enfold us in his love and care for the whole of the day ahead. Each morning we can re-dedicate ourselves to him, give ourselves to him completely, asking that he might work within us, guiding and directing our thoughts and feelings, words and actions throughout the day. We can ask that he might make us one of his instruments for the spreading of love and peace in the world. 'Lord, make me an instrument of thy peace; where there is hatred let me sow love ...'; one of his beacons to shine light and warmth into someone's heart; one of his 'stained glass windows'; one of his friends. And lastly, we can dedicate our day to him, committing ourselves as far as we are able to his praise and worship. 'This is the day which the Lord hath made; we will rejoice and be glad in it ...' (Ps 118:24) Let us therefore dedicate more time in our lives to sharing with God, that we might at least enter into a full and complete relationship with him.

Every morning put your mind into your heart and stand in the presence of God all the day long.

Wednesday

Moreover, the bread which I will give is my own flesh; I give it for the life of the world. (Jn 6: 51)

Reading: Jn 6: 51-58

Here Jesus, speaking to the people of Capernaum, makes reference to his coming sacrifice for the spiritual transformation of humanity. They do not know that he will be put to death within a short space of time, and that it will be, in part, for their sake. They do not understand his words, querying, 'How can this man give us his flesh to eat?' They do not realise that Jesus is speaking through symbolism.

What Jesus is saying to these people, and to us, is that to have greater access to unceasing communion with God, to eternal life, we need to 'ingest' him, that is, to take him into ourselves, deeply and completely, on a spiritual level, and allow him to work fully within us in a transformational manner. 'As the living Father sent me, and I live because of the Father' – because the Father and he are one in the Spirit; 'So he who eats me shall live because of me' – so anyone consciously receiving him into him or her self on a spiritual level, will be enfolded into limitless oneness of the Spirit. 'From him we come, in him we are enfolded, to him we return.' Christ Jesus tells the people of Capernaum, and ourselves: 'My flesh is real food' – his presence within us is real spiritual sustenance; 'my blood is real drink' – his spirit within us is a powerful, inspiring, creative force; 'whoever eats my flesh' – whoever accepts his presence within them and is nourished by it; 'and drinks my blood' – and taps into his inspiring Spirit becoming empowered by the creative impulse within it; 'dwells continually in me and I dwell in him.'

There is another aspect of the words 'flesh' and 'blood' that we might consider. That is that 'my flesh is real food' could be thought of as Christ Jesus' words, the teachings that he gave for us; and 'blood is real drink' could be considered his inspirational thought which manifests in us through our intuition. There are two major areas which we might look at in the gospels relating to these two ideas. The first is what are known as the Beatitudes (Mt 5: 3-12), which summarise many aspects of Jesus' teaching, and the other is the Lord's Prayer (Mt 6: 9-13), that form of prayer

I AM THE BREAD OF LIFE

which Jesus gave to us to help us be attuned more deeply with God. The Beatitudes give us a pattern for living. Within them is contained all that we should strive for as human beings, as children of God, as 'friends' of Christ Jesus. They teach us the importance of peace (v. 9), the need for humility (v. 5), the worth of the search for wisdom (v. 6), the necessity for purity of heart (v. 8); and they give us the promise of future blessings if we work towards all these things.

Secondly, we can look more closely at the Lord's Prayer. We should really try to feel our way into this prayer, rather than simply reciting its words, although it is easy to fall into doing this from force of habit. It is important to say the words slowly and meaningfully, and listen deeply whilst we do. In this way, the Lord's Prayer can become a profound contemplation, a complete meditation in itself, if we dwell meaningfully upon each part of it and listen with our inner ears to God's response coming from the point of stillness within ourselves. 'God is the still point at the centre,' writes Julian of Norwich. It can become a source of spiritual nourishment, a source of intuitive thoughts and feelings about ourselves and God, about our way of doing things in our lives, about what we might do within them for ourselves, for others and for God. So, from that point of stillness within, as we go attentively through the words chosen for us by Christ Jesus, God can reach out and touch our intuition, pouring into our hearts and minds everything that he wants to say to us, and everything that he wants to share with us.

Thus can we see Christ Jesus as our pathway to attunement with God, our pathway to limitless communion with him in his Spirit, both through his 'flesh' – his words and his presence within us, and through his 'blood' – his inspirational thought and his ever empowering Spirit.

For in him we live, and move, and have our being.

Thursday

Everyone who drinks this water will be thirsty again, but whoever drinks the water that I shall give him will never suffer thirst anymore. The water that I shall give him will be an inner spring always welling up for eternal life. (Jn 4: 13-14)

Reading: Jn 4: 1-30

Jesus, coming to a Samaritan town, sits down to rest beside a well. There he meets a Samaritan woman who is surprised by his communication and obvious knowledge of her. Finally he reveals himself to her as the Messiah, offering her 'living water,' that which will be 'always welling up for eternal life.'

As Christ Jesus knew the Samaritan woman intimately, so God in Christ also knows us intimately. He is aware of our every need and has made provision for it. Through prayer, he has given us the chance to come to him and partake of that 'inner spring always welling up for eternal life,' as often and as much as we need. We may, however, sometimes feel that God does not hear us, that he is not aware of our needs and wishes. In these cases our prayer times can become long, repetitive lists of supplications, of requests or demands for God's attention. But he does know, however we may feel about his apparent lack of response. (Mt 6: 33) We should instead, share our needs or requirements and then leave them with him, having faith that he has heard and has 'matters in hand.' We can give him thanks in anticipation of his response, believing in our hearts that he has heard our prayer and is already responding to it in whatever way he knows to be right.

Answers to our prayers may come in different ways from how we expect or hope, as we do not always necessarily know what is really the best for ourselves. So we should not become disheartened if we feel that God is not sending into our lives exactly what we want. He has a deeper understanding of our true needs and an overview of our lives in a way that we do not. What we think is right for us may not in fact be the case. We should try to have faith that God does know best and will send into our lives that which really is right for us, both at the time of asking and also in the long term.

A further occasion for potential disappointment is when we feel that we are experiencing difficulties during our prayer times. However, we should not necessarily expect these to be always comforting, secure and uplifting. We can sometimes experience apparent barrenness or aridity with no feeling of being in God's presence at all. We can also experience pain when something lodged within us comes up to the surface to be healed by God's loving presence.We can also become acutely aware of our imperfections, making us discouraged and loath to keep on trying to come close to God. We feel ourselves to be quite useless or worthless in his eyes. Or sometimes we can just feel unable to pray at all, unable to communicate in any kind of way with God. However, Julian of Norwich speaks of Christ in her vision as saying: 'Pray inwardly, even though you find no joy in it. For it does good, though you feel nothing, see nothing, yes, even though you think you cannot pray. For when you are dry and empty, sick and weak, your prayers please me, though there be little enough to please you. All believing prayer is precious to me.'

So, even though we may feel that we are struggling in our prayer life, we must not allow ourselves to be discouraged as the intention alone will have opened up the channel to God, and he will be responding to us through this. Thus, often, what we consider to have been our least effective prayer times may, in fact, in reality have been our most valuable.

It gives more praise to God and more delight if we pray steadfast in love, trusting his goodness, clinging to him by grace, than if we ask for everything our thoughts can name.

Friday

Whoever believes in me, let him drink. As scripture says, streams of living water shall flow out from within him. (Jn 7: 37-38)

Readings: Jn 7: 37-39 and Ps 84: 6

In these two readings both Christ Jesus himself and the psalmist make reference to the provision of water by God for those needing to quench their thirst. Water is the great medium of cleansing and purification, the great sustainer of life on earth, without it we cannot live. In giving us the image of 'living water,' describing that which God in Christ can provide, they are demonstrating its importance for us. As water is essential for our physical life, so 'living water' is essential for our spiritual life, that 'living water' for which we all thirst, whether we recognise it or not. Christ Jesus offers us a constant supply, from which we may always drink our fill.

However, it seems that if we partake of this 'living water' fully, the result will be that 'streams of living water shall flow out from within', that is we will become channels for this 'living water', this spiritual sustenance flowing from God into the world. We could, therefore, constantly be giving openly and freely of this spiritual sustenance – love, peace and harmony – to others. This would be so if we could come to Christ Jesus and fully partake of this perpetual supply so that we would become filled to the point of overflowing.

There are, however, often obstacles which prevent us from 'overflowing', from 'spilling over' and spreading God's love and harmony in the world. One of these is when we become blocked by resentment, bitterness or repressed anger against others for things which they have done to us in the past. We have held on to these hurts or painful times in our hearts and allowed them to fester and grow worse. The resentment, bitterness or anger gets blocked in and each time we remember the person concerned and the pain they have caused, we add to the severity of the 'wound'. Whilst we continue in this vein the 'wound' will never heal and we will continue to be blocked in by it.

What we do not fully realise is that when our outward-reaching flow is blocked, our inward-filling one can be restricted also. If a

I AM THE BREAD OF LIFE

container is filled to the top and does not spill over it cannot have further in-filling, until more space is made for this to take place. In a similar way, we cannot fully benefit from God's in-flowing of love, harmony and peace into ourselves whilst we are filled with bitterness, anger and old resentments. We need to discard these and make room for positive, healthier thoughts and feelings. We need to throw out all the hate and bring in love in its place.

Christ Jesus says, 'If anyone is thirsty, let him come to me;' – if we 'thirst' for love, peace and harmony in our lives, let us go to Christ Jesus and ask him to help us to forgive. For until we can forgive those who have caused us pain or hardship we cannot truly give freely of ourselves and thereby receive God's love and blessings to the full. However, forgiveness may not come easily to us, depending on how much pain or hardship we have had to suffer through another's actions or words. What we can do is to come to God in prayer and ask him through Christ to open our hearts to those who we feel have wronged us, and to help us to send them thoughts of compassion and forgiveness. This may be difficult to do at first, but with perseverance we can find it easier with God's help. Forgiving and forgetting may not be possible, but forgiving and re-forgiving is. Each time we remember, we can forgive afresh and each time, with help from God, it will become easier.

Making time specifically for forgiving during our prayer times will give us a direct opportunity to work positively in this direction. We can visualise both ourselves and the person concerned together in God's presence. We can 'speak' to them, consciously forgiving them, and asking for forgiveness for ourselves for having directed negativity towards them. At the same time, we can imagine God infusing us both with his healing, harmonising presence. Thus, in this way, God can begin to remove the obstacles within us, enabling us to become clear, free channels into and through which his blessings may flow.

Forgetting those things which are behind and reaching forth unto those things which are before, this is wisdom.

Saturday

Whoever is thirsty, let him come; and whoever wishes, let him take the free gift of the water of life. (Rev 22:17)

Reading: Rev 7: 9-17

John here gives us a vision of those who, having passed through the earthly dimension, have attained sufficient wisdom and spirituality to 'stand before the throne of God and minister to him day and night in his temple' – to be in the ultimate communion with him. We could take this as our ideal, that which we can hope ultimately to attain, that which we can continue to strive for throughout our lives. For these people will be guided to the 'springs of the water of life' by 'the Lamb', their shepherd – he who has offered himself to us in the same role for the same purpose. They are guided by him to the water in the heavenly spheres and we are guided to that same water in the earthly one, with a 'hope of glory' (Col 1:27) to come, a hope that finally he will be able to lead us to the water in the heavenly spheres as well.

Prayer is the means by which we can take up his offer and be guided by him, as our shepherd, to this water of life. It is the means by which we can begin to 'wash our robes and make them white in the blood of the Lamb' – to cleanse ourselves on a soul level through uniting with Christ's Spirit and allowing him to permeate and pervade us on this level until we are purified. Then, through God's grace, can we, his children, move into closer union with him.

For much of the time in our lives we can feel 'empty', devoid of something necessary for our true fulfilment, but somehow not sure what it is or how or where to find it. We can move into certain areas of experience and find temporary fulfilment, a temporary easing of our soul's searching, but it does not really last long and soon we are feeling restless again. Until we come to a full realisation that our souls will never find peace or harmony until they rest in the presence of God and are united with him, our searching for true spiritual fulfilment will remain fruitless. Julian of Norwich says, 'This is the cause why we are not at rest in heart and soul: that here we seek rest in things that are so little there is no rest in them, and we do not know our God who is all mighty, all wise and all good. For he is true rest. No soul can have rest until it

I AM THE BREAD OF LIFE

finds created things are empty. When the soul gives up all for love, so that it can have him that is all, then it finds true rest.'

We spend much of our time seeking fulfilment in our physical world, which does contain within it much of great beauty. However, everything in our physical world is a mere reflection of that which is in God's heaven, and of him who created it. We keep looking to the reflection for fulfilment, for upliftment, for 'rest', instead of looking to that of which, of whom, it is a reflection. If we take a beautiful rose and hold it up to a mirror, within the mirror we will see an object of great loveliness. Yet we can only see it. We cannot savour its fragrance, touch its petals, experience it in its entirety. The reflection which we see is just a small part of its full beauty. This is so with God. We see his reflection everywhere in our world and in our fellow human beings. We sense his presence all round us. But, until we seek him in our soul life 'face to face', we will never experience that sense of completeness, that nourishment of the soul which we so need. Julian says, 'The best prayer is to rest in the goodness of God, knowing that that goodness can reach right down to our lowest depths of need.'

So, in our prayer times it is essential for our well-being that we reach deeply into the silence within us, into the stillness of God's presence where our souls can find the peace and tranquillity which they need, where they can 'rest' in God's compassionate love, and where they can partake of the 'springs of the water of life', as they lie deeply within his Spirit.

Our soul rests in God, its true peace; our soul stands in God, its true strength, and is deep-rooted in God for endless love.

Palm Sunday

Here is your king, who comes to you in gentleness, riding on an ass, riding on the foal of a beast of burden. (Mt 21:5)

Reading: Mt 21: 1-9

Here we see Jesus' entry into Jerusalem, a triumphal entry – the day which we now call Palm Sunday. The people were following him shouting, 'Hosanna to the Son of David!' They were going on before him, throwing down at the feet of his donkey palm branches taken from the nearby trees to make a carpet for him to ride over. Some even added their over-garments. Jesus was being hailed and proclaimed a king. The mood was one of anticipation, excitement and joy. Here was their king who might well liberate them from their oppressors, the Romans, whose presence was heavily felt and much resented. The world was at his feet.

It must have been a similar experience as when Jesus was given the last of his temptations in the wilderness, 'All these I will give you if you will only fall down and do me homage.' (Mt 4:9) His head could have been turned completely and he could have gone forward enjoying the attention directed towards his ego. However, these moments must instead have been bitter-sweet to him for he would have known that the mass hysteria of the moment, the devotion, the attention and the accolade that he was now receiving would have been short-lived; within a very short time the cry of 'Hosanna' would have turned into the cry of 'Crucify'. For many here on this day, the devotion and attention would have turned to derision and aggression towards him. When they realised that his way of liberation was different from what they were expecting – an aggressive overthrow of their Roman oppressors – and was a way of peace and acceptance, they would turn away from him in frustration and resentment. Some would remain faithful and loyal, recognising Jesus for who and what he was and realising what he was trying to teach. Some, already made uncomfortable by the miracles – suspicious magic? – would be easily persuaded by the authorities that he was a dangerous, dishonest or ineffectual man, no longer their king in any form or way.

It is good to remember how easily our emotions can be whipped up in different situations, both negatively and positively. They can distort our vision of something and make us act in ways that are alien to our true perception of a situation, which, if we sit down and think about it afterwards, would seem so obvious. Many times is it possible to do something impulsively because of being emotionally highly charged – and many times we can regret this, whether it is being over-enthusiastic about something at one end of the scale or losing one's temper at the other – just think of what can happen at football matches. It is always necessary to strike a balance, if possible, and keep an awareness that our emotions can play games with us and take us along paths or into situations that we did not intend; or that they can distort our vision so that we get swayed by the mood of the moment into whatever the mass mood happens to be, so that we are not capable of making a fair judgement or assessment of a person or situation.

Christ Jesus was well aware of all this, and is completely aware of it in ourselves today. Often if we are in an emotionally charged state, a little warning bell will ring, a few words will resound in our inner ear reminding us of the necessity for calm assessment or cautious consideration, or just to be realistic about something, when in the excitement of the moment we have let ourselves get carried away and been over-enthusiastic. This is not to criticise spontaneity, for spontaneity is positive and creative and much fruitfulness and joy can be experienced through it.

So Jesus makes his triumphal entry into Jerusalem in gentleness and humility, choosing for his mount a humble donkey and honouring this gentle creature by so doing. He shows us the folly of basking in ego-flattery and hero-worship and reminds us of how a truly gracious and noble king conducts himself. Will we allow him in graciousness, gentleness and humility to make a triumphal entry into our lives?

May Christ Jesus, all compassionate, all loving,
enter our hearts in triumph and grace.

Monday

My house will be called a house of prayer; but you are making it a 'den of robbers'. (Mt 21:13)

Reading: Mt 21: 10-13

So after the triumphal entry into Jerusalem with the crowd 'wild with excitement' Jesus goes to the temple. This is one of the few times in the gospels that we see him expressing anger, righteous anger, at what was happening within the house of God. Money-changers and dealers were making dishonest profits out of innocent pilgrims – the whole system had become corrupt and dishonest. Jesus expresses his anger at the tainting of the holy place by this corruption to which the authorities turned a blind eye. So he goes in and upturns the money-changers' tables; he drives out those buying and selling in the precincts; he clears the 'dross' from the temple in an attempt to cleanse and purify it. He cleanses the outer precincts by physical means in preparation for a 'spiritual' cleansing within during the days to come – the teachings he will bring to them of the kingdom of God.

St Paul tells us that we are all temples for the indwelling Spirit of God. 'Surely you know that you are God's temple, where the spirit of God dwells ... the temple of God is holy; and that temple you are.' (1 Cor 3:16-17) We should try to keep an awareness of this and the self-responsibility that it brings. It is up to each one of us to keep our physical bodies healthy, not to abuse them with excess or to deprive them of what they need for optimum functioning. Preventive 'medicine' is better than curative 'medicine' wherever possible. Our minds too need to be attended to: rested – not overloaded with too many unnecessary or minor daily details; calm – in daily communion with God, even if for just a few minutes; positive – with recognition and thankfulness for all that God provides for us; joyful – through an appreciation of his many wonderful gifts, both to humanity and to us individually.

It is a great gift in itself to be a temple for God's indwelling Spirit. We should allow Christ Jesus to cleanse and purify our 'temple' as he did the temple in Jerusalem, and as he later did, symbolically, his disciples at the Last Supper. (Jn 13: 3-17) There he took water and washed their feet, each of them in turn. While cleansing them on a physical level he symbolically showed them the necessity for spiritual cleanliness. He offered them, and offers us, cleansing and purification on a higher level if we allow his Spirit to flow through us, cleansing even our souls. If we can allow him to flow through us completely, letting go of the many things which block us in our lives, he can, like a river, flow through us, taking obstacles and tensions away and washing us pure and clean on a soul level. St Bernard suggests that water that does not flow stagnates in holes and pools and become full of impurities. We should take care to allow Christ to flow continuously through us so that we give out the love and care with which he fills us to others, that they might share in it. Otherwise it might stagnate into pools of selfishness or self-centredness.

God's Spirit dwelling in us is one of great beauty. Our 'temples' could all be reflections of that beauty. There are certain people that one meets in one's life whose constant infilling and out-giving of God's love are a continual source of inspiration and happiness to those whom they meet. We feel good from having spent time in their presence, and are encouraged to go positively forward in our own lives. Their outer temples reflect the beauty and quality of love of that which dwells in them. God has 'sculpted' them, refined away the dross until the end product gleams with light. A certain sculptor wished to capture the essence of the 'bird' in bronze. After various versions he arrived at a simplified, abstracted shape which had all the essential bird-like qualities contained within it, with no unnecessary details. He cast it and had it polished until it shone. It stood there in purity – the true essence of 'bird', flawless and gleaming.

This can be God's ideal for us, refining us and chipping away at the dross until we are seen in our true, pure, spiritual essence. Let us allow him to work in us and with us until our 'temples' become reflections of the pure Spirit which dwells in them.

Our soul is created to be God's home, and the soul is at home in the uncreated God.

Tuesday

Day by day he taught in the temple. (Lk 19:47)
Reading: Mt 21: 14-17

So after the storming of the temple precincts, Jesus now concentrates on healing the sick and needy. 'Blind men and cripples came to him, and he healed them.' However, it was not enough just to make whole their sick bodies, he also had to nourish and make whole their minds and souls. So his symbolic cleansing of the temple precincts was followed in the days to come by a cleansing within. 'Day by day he taught in the temple. And the chief priests and lawyers were bent on making an end of him with the support of the leading citizens, but found they were helpless, because the people all hung upon his words.' (Lk 19: 47-8) He offered new light on the scripture, in danger of becoming obscure and ossified. He revitalised and clarified the texts through his vigour and conviction. However, it was not just theoretical or rhetorical scripture, it was its practical application. Words were followed up by actions – here was love and compassion personified.

There was an immediacy about Jesus. His very presence, the words he spoke, his compassionate actions convinced and inspired his listeners. Here was a living example of the love, care and compassion of his Father, of their Father, of whom he spoke so much. Blind eyes were opened, inner awareness was increased. Immobile limbs were restored, rigid minds were expanded. Bodies were invigorated, souls were inspired. Negative habitual thought patterns were released making way for new, loving and expansive ones. There was a stirring of bodies, minds and souls as a new force, a new energy penetrated them, one composed of love, forgiveness and compassion on an earthly level, and on a spiritual one, the means for a new relationship with their God. As he healed their sick and crippled bodies through his hands, so too he healed their inner blindness and sickness.

Unlike those people in the temple, we do not have Christ Jesus to come to and ask him to lay his hands upon us and heal us. Yet he made provision for this when he left his earthly ministry. Apart from giving each of us the capacity for self-healing by attuning to his presence working within us, he also gave to his disciples the ability to continue his healing work. Instances are quoted in the

Acts of the Apostles where the apostles minister to sick people and they are healed. Today the Ministry of Healing reaches out and touches many people. Laying on of hands healing is being made available to more and more people in need – and more people are coming to participate in both the giving and receiving of this gift. Healing services are being held in many places, either on a regular basis or as a special event. Clergy and lay people work together in this, facilitating the flow of the healing power of God in Christ into those wishing to benefit from it. People are invited to come not only to receive it for themselves but also on behalf of others in need of help. The person carrying out the laying on of hands calls in prayer upon God in Christ to flow into the person receiving, to enfold them with love and to fill them with healing power that they might be restored to health and wholeness in all parts of their being. Many feel benefit immediately, experiencing relief from pain or tension. Others are given courage and hope that, through receiving healing, and by moving forward in faith, their bodies or minds will be assisted in their own self-healing process over a period of time.

Some deep-rooted illnesses may need time to clear completely, depending upon the circumstances. However, even these can go within a relatively short space of time if there is nothing impeding the healing process. For sometimes the power of healing is not fully effective until we put right certain negative situations or conditions in our lives which block its flow – for example, feelings towards someone which need to be changed. Once these situations have been put right or negative feelings been transformed into loving ones, the gift of the healing power of Christ can flow into and through us to optimum effect and we can receive into our lives the benefits that this brings.

You are our strength, Lord, the source of all healing.
Enfold us in your loving arms that we may be made whole.

Wednesday

In truth, in very truth I tell you, one of you is going to betray me. (Jn 13:21)

Reading: Mk 14: 1-11

There is a certain poignancy in this text, in the contrast between the attitudes to Jesus of Judas and the unnamed woman who brought the gift of costly perfume. Judas could be said to have had 'everything'. He was one of Jesus' close friends, one of the twelve disciples chosen by Jesus to work with him. He spent much of his time in Jesus' presence and was able at close hand to benefit from his teaching and example. Judas carried out a responsible job within the group and in this area held Jesus' trust. Yet, he who had 'everything' threw it away. He betrayed the man who gave him more than any other could.

In contrast, the woman who brought the gift had 'little' by comparison – even if she is the Mary of St John's gospel. (Jn 12: 3-8) Being a woman, the same opportunities were not open to her as Judas – she did not have the chance of a responsible position within Jesus' group of disciples. More importantly, she could not benefit from close, consistent contact with Jesus. Yet she came in humility and gave to him 'everything' in her one act, her gift of anointing – love, devotion, service, thankfulness, loyalty. She who had little gave everything. He who had much threw it away. Thus, Jesus, knowing the course events would take, received the wound of pending betrayal from his close friend yet, at the same time, received for this wound salve from the love and loyalty of an unnamed devotee.

Could we say of these two people that the one made the most of her one opportunity and the other took what he had for granted? For it does seem that what Judas had was not enough for him. We do not know exactly why he betrayed Jesus. Perhaps he was frustrated by what he felt was Jesus' wasted opportunity to take power when he entered Jerusalem. Perhaps he became disillusioned by Jesus' teaching, 'knowing' the ways of men and women too well to think that they could change their ways. Perhaps he genuinely wanted some of the Roman injustices put right and thought to force Jesus' hand by handing him over to the authorities. Or perhaps he wanted power and used this as a means of getting it. Whatever the reason, Judas must have been dissatisfied

BEHOLD THE LAMB OF GOD

with what he had – and yet he had so much.

When we are frustrated by events in our lives, or disillusioned, when we feel cynical or resentful about things, do we blame it all on God? Do we try to force his hand? Do we turn our back on him? Do we take for granted all the positive elements in our lives and just focus on the negative ones? Are we really grateful enough for what we have?

The woman in the reading, on the other hand, was grateful for the little that she had – the opportunity to give to the person to whom she was devoted something of great cost to herself, and in the giving of it, the chance to express all her gratitude to him in one great act of love and devotion. Jesus acknowledges her gratitude towards him and the greatness of her gift: 'I tell you this: wherever in all the world the Gospel is proclaimed, what she has done will be told as her memorial.'

St Luke quotes an instance when Jesus is met by ten lepers, all asking him to take pity on them. (Lk 17:11-19) Jesus sends them to the priests, and on their way, they are healed. Only one thinks to return to say thank you. The others, effectively, take Jesus' gift for granted without thought of expressing any gratitude. Jesus asks where the rest are of those healed, and could they not return to praise God for their gift of wholeness?

How many times do we pray for help in certain situations; ask for guidance in our lives; ask for harmony in particular circumstances; pour out all our troubles, thoughts and feelings, stresses and strains to God and ask him to deliver us from them. But do we always remember to say thank you? Which are we most like – the nine lepers or the one that came back? The unnamed woman or Judas?

Thanksgiving is the deep inward certainty which moves us with reverent and loving fear to turn with all our strength to the work to which God stirs us, giving thanks and praise from the depths of our hearts.

Maundy Thursday

This is my body given for you; do this in remembrance of me. (Lk 22:19)
Readings: Mk 14: 22-25 and 1 Cor 12: 14-31

So we come to the Last Supper, the last time Jesus would share a supper with his disciples prior to his arrest and trial. It was a pre-Passover meal, an intimate gathering, a time of sadness because Jesus knew that he would not share the Passover itself with them. Yet, it was also a time of great love and compassion as Jesus shared many deep thoughts, feelings and teachings with them, comforting them with the promise of the Holy Spirit who would come to be with them in his place. Most of his disciples, however, did not even then fully realise that he would, in a short while, no longer be with them.

During the supper he took a loaf of unleavened bread, blessed it and broke it up, giving some to each disciple: 'Take this; this is my body.' Many symbolic references were contained within this gesture. It heralded his coming sacrifice, when his physical body would be broken up in order that they, and humanity as a whole, might spiritually take a step closer to their Creator. The blessing of the bread not only purified and sanctified it through God's presence within it, but also represented the purification and sanctification of Jesus' own body through his ultimate sacrifice. The distribution, the giving of the bread to the disciples, the sharing in the one loaf which symbolised himself, represented the sharing of himself with his disciples and with humanity as a whole, in a different form. 'This is my body, broken for you, bringing you wholeness, making you free, take it and eat it, and when you do, do it in love for me.'

Then he took a cup, blessed it and passed it round for all to drink from it. 'This is my blood... shed for many ...' – the blood which symbolised the life-force which would flow out from him, causing him deep suffering, so that humanity might be sustained, nourished and empowered by the gift of infusion of his Spirit. 'This is my blood, poured out for you, bringing forgiveness, making you free, take it and drink it, and when you do, do it in love for me.'

For through Christ Jesus' death, through the sharing of his body and blood, we all became part of a single body. Through his death, his body was broken, symbolically, into innumerable parts, as many as there are people on earth. We corporately share in his body, but it is a spiritual sharing rather than a corporeal one. For we were all included in the Last Supper, we have all taken part in it by inference and are still part of it now. 'This is my blood ... shed for many' – this means all of us. Christ Jesus, in sacrificing himself for us, gave us a promise: that we would all, from that time onwards, have the provision, through grace, to come spiritually closer to God. And he bound us closely together through himself so that we might feel ourselves to be one, all part of the whole, linked by him and in him wherever and whoever we may be.

'For Christ is like a single body with its many limbs and organs, which many as they are, together make up one body.' (1 Cor 12: 12) If we think of the workings of our own bodies we will see that all parts play their part in the harmonious functioning of the whole organism, and that what affects one part can also affect a number of others. 'Now you are Christ's body, and each of you a limb or organ of it.' We each have our individual skills and gifts to offer one another, and from which each of us can benefit. We must be prepared to share with each other – to experience together our joys and sorrows; to uplift and inspire one another; to console and empathise; to understand and forgive. And it must never matter what our backgrounds are, what colour we are, what belief systems we adhere to, what experience of life we have had. We should take care to treat everyone whom we meet similarly – graciously and courteously – making no distinctions between them whatever their walk of life. For we should always look beyond any 'container' to what it contains – and we all contain the Spirit of God.

Though we are many, we are one body,
because we all share in one bread.

Good Friday
Behold the Man. (Jn 19:5)
Reading: Jn 19: 17-30

These were the last few agonising hours. The 'trials' were completed and Jesus had been handed over to the soldiers to be crucified. He had worked tirelessly for his Father and brought to fruition all that had been planned for him. He had known, in all that time, that it would eventually mean the giving of his life in order that the divine will might be fulfilled. These were his last few hours – hours of agony and grief, but also of triumph.

He was to offer his greatest gift, the ultimate gift that he, Christ Jesus, could bring to his Father, could bring to us all. He would lay aside his ego; he would submit to the divine will and give up his body and his spirit for the spiritual development of humanity, thereby facilitating our steps towards spiritual enlightenment and a closer relationship with God. And he would also bind us together spiritually as a whole within himself.

He showed us by example what we must do, symbolically, in our own lives. As he laid down his life and being to God for our sake, so we must lay down ourselves and our lives to God, for his. As he laid aside his ego and submitted to the divine will, so should we lay aside our ego desires, our ego promptings, and submit to the divine will in our lives. Lent is a good time to take stock of ourselves, review immediate past events and those which occurred further back in our past. We can look back and see if we have learned from them. We might follow the old custom of 'giving something up for Lent' to remind ourselves, symbolically, that there may be many things which we need to lay aside in order to move forward in our lives.

We should each submit ourselves to God's purpose for us rather than tell him what is best for us, and what we want out of life. We should not make our own ego desires into our god. It may not, at times, be easy to see what God has in store for us, or what purpose there is in the situations and events that we experience. Yet God does have his purpose for us; he does have his reasons for us being where we are, for things happening in the way that they do, even though it may not be clear to us what they are. We can only trust in his goodness and have faith. We can look to Mary, the mother of Jesus, for help in this. She submitted to God's will in his great task for her, to bear our Saviour – 'Here am I, I am the Lord's servant; as you have spoken, so be it.' (Lk 1:38) Christ Jesus acknowledges her great gift to him and to the world and her ultimate submission to God's will when, from the cross, he entrusts her into the care of his beloved disciple.

For even in the hours of his greatest suffering, Christ Jesus considered others rather than himself, laying aside his own pain in the fulfilment of his Father's will, that of showing love and compassion, forgiveness and understanding to all his people. He showed compassion to those who wept for him on his way to Golgotha (Lk 23:28-31); he asked forgiveness for those who had condemned, mocked and crucified him (Lk 23:34); and he showed understanding towards those crucified with him. (Lk 23:39-43) Christ Jesus turned to his Father in selflessness in his times of need and suffering, and gave himself up into God's care in faith and trust. He invites us, in our times of hardship, suffering and need, to give ourselves up to him in the same way. (Mt 11:28-9) For he will be present in the midst of our tribulations, in the midst of our suffering, for he has been through the same himself – and he will be in the midst of our pain, sharing and experiencing it with us, for he is within each of us as we are within him. (Jn 14:20) This is his greatest gift to us.

I am thy friend, thy sorrows mine,
and love to share this cross of thine.
I am thy friend.

Holy Saturday

Now at the place where he had been crucified there was a garden, and in the garden a new tomb, not yet used for burial. There, because the tomb was near at hand and it was the eve of the Jewish Sabbath, they laid Jesus. (Jn 19: 41-42)

Reading: Jn 19: 31-42

Now we stand silently with the followers of Jesus beside the tomb. It is not difficult to imagine the thoughts passing through their minds and the atmosphere, heavy with sadness, surrounding them. Everything must have seemed hopeless now with their Master dead. The focus of their lives was gone; their inspiration, their hope was lying in a tomb. They were now alone and directionless, like sheep without a shepherd.

This is something which we all have to face sometime in our lives – bereavement. We can all empathise with how these followers of Jesus felt, believing that they would never see him again. It is one of the most difficult things to come to terms with in our lives, the fact that we will never again see a loved one; hear their familiar voice or laugh; watch their special smile; feel the touch of their hand or their embrace; share with them in all kinds of ways. For people on their own again after many years of close relationship with another, the sense of loss can be devastating. Their way of life can be turned completely upside down. And there are all the immediate concerns to be attended to, one being the task of going through all their loved one's possessions, those objects which have been lovingly gathered and treasured over the years, and which have held special memories for both the loved one individually and for them together.

This can be one of the most difficult things of all to deal with. Yet it can serve two positive purposes. One is that it helps us to grieve, and this is most important. It is not helpful to block off our feelings, to keep a 'stiff upper lip' in times of bereavement. We should allow ourselves to feel and express our grief and pain or else it can get blocked inside and cause us many problems at a later stage, both physical and psychological. It is perfectly right and healthy to express our feelings, our pain, our desolation.

The second positive purpose that it fulfils is that it gives us the chance to perform one last service for our loved one, as did the women who came to Jesus' tomb bringing oils and unguents to offer their one last devotional service for their Master. It gives us the opportunity to offer one final mark of respect, one last gift given in love and thanks for the time spent by our loved one with us. Sorting through and appropriately distributing a person's possessions is something very personal, very close, for one is sharing in the intimate detail of that person's life, their special memories, things that they held dear, items which they chose to use or wear which were reflections of that person as a human being. Loving attention to a person's possessions can be considered an act of respect, an honouring of that person as an individual, a child of God, an acknowledgement of all that they believed in and cared for, of all that they held in esteem and treasured. It is a great privilege to be allowed to share in this.

There is, however, one major difference between our feelings in times of bereavement and those of Jesus' followers. Those people thought that it was the end, that they would never see him again. We know that although we will not see our loved ones again in physical form, they are still with us in a different form as part of God's heavenly kingdom, part of the communion of saints, those who have passed this way before and have now moved closer into God's presence; and that, when the time is right, we will rejoin them. Finally, we know that the death and entombment of Jesus was not in fact the end for them or for us. It is beautifully demonstrated by an anonymous thirteenth century writer:

'Here you are, in tears, outside a tomb. But my tomb is your heart, and there I am not dead, but resting, and alive for all eternity. Your soul is my garden, and you are right to suppose that I am the gardener. I am the new Adam, and I both care for my paradise and protect it.'

Rest in peace, sacred body, for which I no longer shall weep.
Rest in peace and bring rest to me also.
The tomb which is destined for you no longer holds suffering,
For me it opens heaven and closes hell.

Easter Sunday

I am he that liveth, and was dead; and behold I am alive for evermore.' (Rev 1: 18)

Reading: Jn 20

The day of the Resurrection has dawned. The tomb is empty. Christ Jesus has conquered death; he has broken through the bonds of the physical kingdoms. He has burst forth from the tomb.

A butterfly, when its time has come, breaks forth from the 'tomb' of its encasing chrysalis. Mysteriously, it has been transformed into a new and glowing creature. God has freed it from its earthly limitations; it has passed through a 'veil' and burst forth into a new dimension. Through the mystery of the resurrection, Christ has released us from the bonds of our physical existence so that we can, with him, leap up from out of our earthly bodies and more easily pass through the 'veil' of death into the spiritual kingdom, when our time comes. 'They cut me down and I leapt up high. I am the life that'll never, never die.'

All life is a dance – a sacred dance, offered to God, contained within God and containing him. Sometimes we spiral around on our own; sometimes we are partnered or in a circle, facing one another or following. The sacred dance of life is one of continuous movement; things cannot remain static, 'preserved' in one particular state. Our journey through life must be one of movement and growth. Christ wants us to flow with him into and through different experiences, to continually enrich our 'dance'. He asks us to 'let go'; to surrender ourselves completely to his love and to the divine will; to liberate ourselves through him; to flow with him and to 'dance' with him. 'Dance, then, wherever you may be. I am the Lord of the Dance, said he, and I'll lead you all wherever you may be, and I'll lead you all in the dance, said he.' Let us take up this offer. Let us all join hands and, with Christ Jesus as leader in our midst, let us dance the sacred dance of life together.

Be assured, I am with you always, to the end of time.